"Julia Loren is a skilled, anointed author and I love her books! They are always relevant, scripturally sound and current to what God is saying to His Church. I was deeply encouraged in my faith when I read *When God Says Yes!* You will be, too."

—Patricia King, www.XPmedia.com

"Once again Julia Loren has done an extraordinary job of capturing end-of-the-age truth and articulating it in clear and concise ways that make it practical and empowering. Many credible prophetic voices are emerging today with biblical insights that identify our place in Church history, along with the mobilization of a company of people to cooperate with God to see His mandates completed. This book is one such tool. I recommend the truth of this book to every hungry believer aspiring to walk with God intimately and to function in the miraculous demonstration of the Holy Spirit to reap the greatest harvest of all time."

—Paul Keith Davis, founder, WhiteDove Ministries; www.whitedoveministries.org

"Stories frame our lives, birth our passions, even affect our concept of God. Julia Loren takes stories, both glad and sad, and weaves them masterfully into tapestries heralding the love of God, as well as our faith and hope in Him. Hold onto your seat as you travel through this book—gripping at times, funny at others and always undergirded with the assurance of God's goodness. I love this book; it is so human yet so divine. It makes God real in the midst of life's happenings."

—Barbara J. Yoder, senior pastor and lead apostle, Shekinah Christian Church; founder and apostolic leader, Breakthrough Apostolic Ministries Network; chancellor, Breakthrough Leadership Institute; www.shekinahchurch.org; www.barbarayoderblog.com

"Julia Loren, in her book *When God Says Yes*, has written a masterpiece that will inspire you to live the abundant life of God's overwhelming supernatural provision. You will gain access to the secrets of obtaining every one of God's promises and will come to see and know the God of more than enough! Get ready to experience the blessed life God has for you."

—Matt Sorger, Matt Sorger Ministries; host, *Power for Life*; www.mattsorger.com

"Be prepared to move into deeper realms of trusting God. Julia Loren has gathered a 'great cloud of witnesses' that will cheer you on in your journey into His heart. I thoroughly enjoy Julia's unique writing style. She captures life in a way that throbs with courage, compassion, humor and heart. As I read, cried and laughed through each chapter, my heart was brought into deeper places of joyful confidence in our faithful Abba."

—Dave Hess, senior pastor, Christ Community Church (Camp Hill, PA); author, *Hope Beyond Reason*

"Such an engaging read. As a counselor and teacher on money, stewardship and the supernatural promises of the Bible, I am continually searching for authors who capture the spirit and truth of God's Word on the topic of provision. This book makes my recommended reading list! Julia has done a tremendous service to the Body of Christ and to all who seek truth about the God we serve. As a gentle and intelligent storyteller, Julia reminds us of a greater reality, brushing our faces against the mighty Kingdom of heaven. Refreshing, elegant and thought-provoking, this book is a reminder of how, even in challenges, God continues to say yes."

—Stephen DeSilva, CPA, CFO, Bethel Church (Redding, CA)

"Julia has married the truth of Scripture and life-changing encounters to produce a text that truly has texture. This book will be a transfusion of hope to those whose faith has become anemic. Your faith will be bolstered to cling to God's promises in the face of any contradiction."

—Randall Worley, Ph.D., founder, Headwaters Ministries; www.hwministries.com

"Julia lives a contagious life, and this latest work of hers, *When God Says Yes*, will infect your life with irreparable courage! She has managed to leave markers on a trail she and her friends have traversed that will lead you to a deeper trust in God for the impossible. These testimonies are power-packed God encounters that point the way to prosperous living. They are gripping because they are real, born out of authentic life struggles, its valleys and, in some cases, raw pain. They point the way for any pilgrim journeying to the high places in search of victory. You will find new wind for your sails by what you discover within these pages. This is truly a great read!"

—Pastors Kim and Mary Andersson, Christ the Rock Ministries of Northern California

"Of all of Julia's books, I like this one best. *Oh wait, I said that about the last one . . . and the one before!*"

—Caroline Loren, Julia's mother

# WHEN GOD
## SAYS YES

# WHEN GOD SAYS YES

His Promise and Provision
When You Need It Most

## JULIA C. LOREN

**Chosen**

*a division of Baker Publishing Group*
Grand Rapids, Michigan

Published by Chosen Books
a division of Baker Publishing Group
P.O. Box 6287, Grand Rapids, MI 49516-6287
www.chosenbooks.com

Printed in the United States of America

Library of Congress Cataloging-in-Publication Data
Loren, Julia C.
    When God says yes : His promise and provision when you need it most / Julia C. Loren.
        p.    cm.
    Includes bibliographical references.
    ISBN 978-0-8007-9486-6 (pbk.)
    1. Prayer—Christianity. 2. Miracles. 3. God (Christianity)—Promises. I. Title.
BV220.L67  2010
231.7—dc22                                                          2009038078

10   11   12   13   14   15   16        7   6   5   4   3   2   1

God is able to make all grace abound to you,
so that always having all sufficiency in everything,
you may have an abundance for every good deed.

2 Corinthians 9:8, NASB

# CONTENTS

Acknowledgments   11
Foreword by James W. Goll   13
Tune In to the Miraculous   15

 1   He Hears Your Whispered Prayers   25
 2   Living on the Currency of God's Love   37
 3   Angels Watching over You   57
 4   Hope beyond Reason for Healing   79
 5   Reclaiming Faith after Heartache   97
 6   He Crowns Your Family with Salvation   113
 7   The Blessing of Childlike Faith   133
 8   Recovering Commitments to Marriage and
       Ministry   149
 9   Stumbling into Destiny   169
10   Experiencing God's Financial Miracles   187

Afterword: The Secret to Sustaining Faith   207
Notes   215

# ACKNOWLEDGMENTS

**Special Thanks To:**

Karen and Carl Berner—for your ongoing friendship and being so encouraging and supportive of me during this crazy, peripatetic phase of my writing.

Melinda and Bard Rice—for graciously lending me your Lake Tahoe getaway, where I wrote half the book.

YWAM's Springs of Living Waters Conference Center in Chico, California—for hosting me in such a peaceful, Spirit-filled atmosphere while I wrote the rest of the book.

Richere Lydon of the Jelly Belly Candy Company—who, having heard that I keep a dish of Jelly Bellies handy while I write, gave me a huge supply (including my favorite—sours) and let me test drive the power beans when I needed them most.

And last but far from least: Jane Campbell of Chosen Books—for believing in me and giving me an opportunity to expand my publishing horizons and blow the kisses of God to the world through this book.

# FOREWORD

Have you ever gone out in the middle of the night and looked up at the vast display of stars shining ever so brightly, looking down just on you, and been awed? I have. In fact, I often go out at night, sit in our green, wooden porch swing overlooking the rolling hills of Franklin, Tennessee, and just look up and ponder on God's majesty.

In such experiences, you can either feel so little and lost that you wonder if God even knows your name and address (I have done that also), or you can sense and know His great, deep love and have an epiphany in which you become more aware that you are not just another speck in the cosmic array of things. You are the very object of His delight, and God has a definite "Yes" in His heart concerning you, your life and His promises. After all, the promises of God are "Yes and Amen" for those who are in Christ Jesus! Hopefully, that includes you.

My friend Julia Loren brings a diverse background of skills to the plate when she writes. Not only are her writings grounded in Scripture, but they also carry a depth of understanding about the human makeup from her psychological training. On top of that, her gleanings are full of verifiable modern-day testimonies—God Stories—from many of our mutual friends.

As you read *When God Says Yes*, you will be exposed to a plethora of small and great things the Lord has done in our day. You will be encouraged to know that the same God who created the universe also delights in listening to your whispered prayers. You will be touched by the Papa heart of God and know that you are really, really, really not alone— angels are watching out after you! Julia helps you return to the curiosity of a childlike heart, where all things are new and marvelous, where you can make mistakes and still stumble into destiny knocking at your door.

Been at wits' end? I have in recent days and months, and I have been at this Spirit-filled evangelical walk for over thirty years! But Julia takes us past the temporary valleys of disappointment and shows us that hope is our next appointment in God. You, too, can reclaim faith even after heartache or receive hope that goes beyond reason. You, too, can arise and say along with me, "The best is yet to come!"

Join with me in the journey of God's heart that has a "Yes and Amen" in it even toward you! Join me as I go out and take a view of the heavens on a southern, starlit night and declare, "God Says Yes!"

With anticipation,
Dr. James W. Goll
Encounters Network • Prayer Storm • Compassion Acts

# TUNE IN TO THE MIRACULOUS

I was raised in a wealthy neighborhood, although my parents were not wealthy and all that they had drained away through time and troubles. By the time I graduated from high school, we had lost everything. In the meanwhile, I saw men chase wealth, become millionaires, lose it all in a week, then slowly regain the illusion of wealth solely by their wits and their gift for business. Their wives retreated to spas, lost themselves in antianxiety medications and searched for cosmetic fixes that would erase every sign of aging. Their children, my peers, ran wild along the oceanfront, hosted lavish parties while their parents were out of town and delighted to take their parents' lifestyles to the next level of prosperity—or at least live off the trust funds for the rest of their lazy and aimless lives. They played while I worked any job I could to help us keep our home. I worked alongside my father painting houses, or closer to home as a babysitter. We lived like immigrants striving to lay hold of the American dream, or at least vainly attempting to maintain what we had.

The recession of the 1970s hit us hard. My parents' marriage almost did not make it. They let go of the house and their neighborhood, stopped trying to keep up with the

Joneses and tumbled into a less prosperous illusion. Along the way, I learned how quickly life can squash one person and elevate another to the heights of prosperity. Eventually, I would learn that although life is hard at times, God is always good and always provides. He provides beyond wealth.

Our ideas of provision and prosperity are usually shaped during childhood and reinforced by how our parents raised us and handled their own finances. I walked into adulthood caring little about becoming wealthy. Having become a Christian, I thought it more important to focus on building the Kingdom of heaven rather than prospering here on earth and storing up wealth for retirement. My idealism was not tempered by wisdom. And I struggled often with envy and shame that I should be so poor while others, who cared little about God, became really comfortable and rich in life, acquiring lots of things.

I have struggled financially most of the years of my life, as have many of you. But God has always come through. Along the way, God has prospered me in many ways and has taught me a few things about appropriating His promises in Scripture. He has taught me about the true meaning of prosperity and how to experience His miraculous provision. Along the way, God has taught me to tune in to the miraculous, pay attention and learn to receive more.

God's intent is that we should prosper even as our souls prosper (see 3 John 1:2). He intends that we have enough to give a "good measure" (see Luke 6:38) and hold it loosely enough so that if the Holy Spirit moves us to give it all away, we have confidence that God will provide abundantly. We learn to live large on the currency of grace and love as Christians, no matter how much money we have in the bank or how many toys are stored in the garage. We learn that when there is no food in the pantry or the refrigerator, God comes through. We watch and stand amazed that He is not stingy, but knows our whispered prayers and the longing of our hearts. He runs to meet us in ways that money cannot buy. And as we join our hearts and minds to His value system, we learn that He always gives more than enough for us to give away.

In the in-between times, when it seems as though there is barely enough and God has forgotten you, when you anxiously stare into the darkness of your desperation and wonder when you will have more than enough money in the bank and food in the pantry to give away, hold onto this thought:

---

## *Promise*

*God's grace will abound to you.*

---

God is able to make all grace abound to you, so that always having all sufficiency in everything, you may have an abundance for every good deed.

2 Corinthians 9:8, NASB

God knows your circumstances and is more than capable of providing more than you ask for. His provision is nothing short of miraculous at times. His intent is to prosper you emotionally, physically and materially. Along the way, He wants to reveal the secrets to appropriating more of His promises and receiving more of His miraculous provision.

### Strategies for Provision

"As he [any person] thinks in his heart, so *is* he" (Proverbs 23:7, NKJV). When I tune in to the promises of God, my whole thought life becomes transformed. When I tune in to my negative, hopeless thoughts on any given day, it is no surprise that I spiral into a pit of depression. However, when I pick up the Word and one of God's promises leaps off the page and into my heart, I begin to soar with hope and joy. Thoughts precede action. If I think that God does not care and will not come through for me, then I operate in unbelief. God is not attracted to unbelief; He is attracted to faith. In the Word, His miracles manifested most to the ones who approached Jesus in faith; not unbelief.

God works to stir up faith in us and help us both to believe in Jesus and to overcome our unbelief. And some days, when deadlines loom and anxiety spills over into unbelief, it takes work to believe that Jesus will meet our needs. It takes work to believe that His promises and provision will come when we need it most.

What we do with God's promises affects our thought lives and our actions. Often, I find a promise and wait in faith-full expectation. Sometimes the provision attached to that promise does not manifest in my reality until years later. Other times, the answer comes instantly; even while I am thinking thoughts of faith. And often, the promise leads me to ask for a strategy to reach out for the provision.

Many of the strategies for receiving God's miraculous provision are ones that you already know but may have forgotten. The first strategy for receiving more from God is to tune in to the miraculous. Drop your focus on the problems and tune in to the times when God met you . . . or at least tune in to the stories of others and let their faith pull yours up a notch or two.

Remembering the times when God met you, when He miraculously provided for you, provides the antidote to anxiety and shifts you from anxiety to faith. Tuning in to the miraculous provision and love and grace that God provides to you on a daily basis involves paying attention, focusing on Him every day. The secret to receiving God's miraculous provision begins with paying attention to what He gives and knowing that it may not come to us all wrapped up in the package we imagined. Miracles are spontaneous events beyond our control. Miracles do not look like we want them to, but the impact is more stunning than we could ever hope or imagine. Miracles are gifts that can appear like tiny flowers in the desert or like pillars of fire lighting up the night. Whether they are small or large, remembering the miracles in your life or surrounding your life makes space in your heart for faith to bloom.

Another strategy for receiving God's provision involves consciously tuning in to God's presence. I am in the habit of daily worship and prayer and have become increasingly interested in tuning in to the miraculous gifts God provides every day. One day, I stumbled

> Miracles are gifts that can appear like tiny flowers in the desert or like pillars of fire lighting up the night.

onto a prayer that God always delights to answer: "Show me something good today, Jesus!" I am not down and depressed when I pray it. I am unabashedly saying, with childlike delight and faith, "Bless me! Provide for me some token of Your miraculous provision, and let me see it happen today!" Yet I am also asking the Lord to show me something of His goodness. I am saying, "Let Your goodness pass before me, and help me make sure my eyes are wide open to see You!"

Most importantly, by praying that prayer, I am setting myself up to be aware of the moment in which He shows me His goodness. Sometimes I write down the story. Sometimes I do not. I am learning to recognize the Lord's hand providing everything and in everyone's lives. I am learning to listen to the way He speaks. And I am also learning to hear His stories spoken in the moment. They are stories that some angel in heaven is probably recording in a book of remembrance and storing in the vaults of heaven. Books of remembrance are mentioned in Scripture. The angels record the stories we miss.

How many times have we heard God's voice, paused to consider if it really was Him talking or just our inner voice and gone on our way without responding? How many times have we witnessed God's extravagant provision and thought that perhaps it was not Him, it was our own strength that worked salvation for us in that circumstance, or our own paycheck earned by the sweat of our efforts?

How many times have we seen where God blessed His people in miraculous and personal ways, both in the Word and in the lives of those surrounding us? All too often, though, we forget what the Lord has done and are swallowed up in self-pity and doubt. Yet others who are wise enough to write their stories can return to the pages of their memories and pull out a few memorial stones.

Setting up memorial stones is another great strategy to help you receive the provision of God. Each recorded memory of when and where God met you becomes a memorial stone that marks where God touched your life. When you are in need of provision, go back and ponder these miraculous events until faith floods your heart once again—faith that God will meet you once again.

Setting up memorial stones is an Old Testament tradition that serves to mark the time and place of God's divine intervention. Markers increase a sense of belonging to Him and make us feel secure in the knowledge that He is our refuge and deliverer. In 1 Samuel 7:12, Samuel "took a stone and set it up between Mizpah and Shen. He named it Ebenezer [which means 'stone of help'], saying, 'Thus far has the LORD helped us.' "

Another biblical account of a memorial stone set up as a monument to the Lord's intervention occurs in the book of Joshua. God miraculously intervened by parting the waters of the Jordan River so the Ark of the Covenant could pass through:

So Joshua called together the twelve men he had appointed from the Israelites, one from each tribe, and said to them, "Go over before the ark of the LORD your God into the middle of the Jordan. Each of you is to take up a stone on his shoulder, according to the number of the tribes of the Israelites, to serve as a sign among you. In the future, when your children ask you, 'What do these stones mean?' tell them that the flow of the Jordan was cut off before the ark of the covenant of the LORD. When it crossed the Jordan, the waters of the Jordan were cut off. These stones are to be a memorial to the people of Israel forever."

Joshua 4:4–7

Write down the times when God met you. Begin collecting your memorial stones of divine intervention and miraculous provision into one place. It will help you stay focused on the Lord and put things in perspective. It will cause you to say, "This is where God met me. He found me and reached out to me. He showed His power and revealed His love. Surely, He will come again. Surely, He has never left me. In fact, I will rejoice in the fact that my Father is deeply concerned with all that concerns me and has plans for a future and a hope for me. I will give thanks and praise that His help will soon be revealed, for He has promised that He will never leave me nor forsake me. I am His beloved, and He is mine."

Every story in the Bible is designed to increase our understanding of God and raise our faith to believe beyond our natural senses. Every single person the Bible mentions personally encountered God. In the Old Testament, every single person standing in a crowd felt the emotional impact when the glory of God showed up. In the New Testament, Jesus impacted every single person in the masses when He ministered, healed and delivered. Whether they stood in a crowd or stood alone before God, Jesus or an angel, each person felt some touch from God. Many were touched by the reading of the Word or by a prophet's words. Others received healing in their diseased bodies. More than one was startled by the sudden appearance of an angel. Both believers and unbelievers found themselves troubled by dreams sent from heaven. Many lapsed into life-changing visions. And a few discovered that their actions transcended the ordinary laws of physics, time and space—that miracles happen and the unexplainable occurs.

God is still touching every single person who comes to Him. And here is an even more outlandish thought: Perhaps God seeks to reveal Himself to us all—whether we seek Him or not. Perhaps God wants to provide miracles every day that provision us for the journey into our destiny.

## Shared Stories

Biblical stories serve to increase our faith that God will walk into our lives in a moment of divine intervention—whether we are ready or not. Faith comes by hearing . . . and reading . . . stories. And meditating on those stories should catapult us into our own stories.

The stories I have included in this book, stories of real people and the provision of God they experienced, also serve as memorial stones stacked in the desert to mark where heaven came to earth in individual lives. Shared stories allow us to draw on one another's breakthroughs. Like Jacob when he encountered the vision of angels ascending and descending, we do not leave a place of visitation without marking it forever in our memory. Jacob left his memorial stones stacked in the desert as a reminder to all pilgrims and passersby that heaven is real and that once upon a time, heaven broke through on that spot.

Our memorial stones are stories as well. Let the stories included in the pages ahead serve as markers for you—signposts that will guide you into your own God encounters. God has never stopped ascending and descending, breaking through the thin veil that divides heaven from earth. He can come to you, too.

The individuals who contributed their stories to this book are ordinary believers like you and me. Some are wives, moms, husbands or businessmen. Others are pastors and prophets and apostles. But even those in ministry today started building their faith through encounters initiated by God.

In this book, leaders like Barbara Yoder share their stories vulnerably and honestly. Their testimonies tell how they encountered God in such a way that hope for the impossible was born, hope that enabled them to hold on until breakthrough happened. As Barbara explains, "We're not God. We're human beings who have been touched with pain and weakness and doubt and unbelief so that people can grab hold of us. If you cannot find God right now, just grab hold of my faith until you can access faith directly yourself."

Grab hold of and draw on their stories; hold onto their faith until faith rises so completely in you that you become fully persuaded that God has the power to do what He promises, even for you. *And especially for you.*

Tune in to the miraculous, and you will soon see that not only has God been providing for you, but He is about to release even more. Expect miracles and you will see them.

# 1

# HE HEARS
# YOUR WHISPERED PRAYERS

I have known extreme poverty and times of great loss, and fleeting though those seasons were, the lessons learned are forever etched upon my softened heart. And at the end of the day, I can say that the lessons revealed a singular truth—life is hard at times, but God hears our whispered prayers and proves it when we least expect it.

One morning I awoke to not a scrap of food in the house. My search of every nook and cranny scrounged up less than a dollar's worth of loose change. That was the day I learned the first of many secrets about God's methods of provision— to tune in to the miraculous. Expect miracles and they will be revealed. However, once the miracles manifest, we must also learn how to receive them.

I had spent the past two years studying journalism at the University of Washington and was forced to take some time off to focus on work before I could be readmitted—forced by finances, for no other reason than lack of funds. As often happens in life, "bad luck" turned even uglier. My roommate moved out, leaving me with double my anticipated rent. My other bills also increased, and paying bills and rent took all that I earned. I could not afford food if I paid rent. Neither could I afford to repay that little $3000 student loan that barred my ability to complete the final eighteen credits I needed to obtain my degree. Day after day, I scrounged around in the cupboards and refrigerator, making meager meals out of plain oatmeal, peanut butter on crackers and top ramen, until one morning I awoke to find that I had exhausted my rations. There was literally not a crumb to eat in the place.

Rather than staring at the walls of my apartment, I decided to take a walk toward the harbor and try to come up with a plan about whom to call for help. I thought the harbor's still waters would help restore peace to my soul. I could not stand the thought of asking for help. My parents stressed self-reliance. They encouraged my education, but they had nothing to put toward funding the venture. I had little contact with relatives and would have died of embarrassment to ask them for help. I had been through terrible emotional times and was reeling from grief and loss in recent years. Facing financial blows seemed like nothing in comparison to working through those emotional disasters, so I was not too worried. Life would work out somehow. After all, in America hunger is optional. A way to access a meal is always available somewhere.

I reached the water's edge and stood for a moment in the chilly air, watching the ducks swimming in the icy water and remembering the Scripture that encourages us not to worry about what to eat or what to wear, since God even clothes the flowers and feeds the birds. He knows what we have need of.

God knows, but do others know? I wondered. Should I call someone from church and hint around at a dinner invitation? Should I call my parents and ask them for some money?

26

For some odd reason, I was ashamed of my poverty. I had been taught by my parents (who were raised in the depression era) that self-reliance was the key to survival. I would survive this season—with God's help. I just had no clue what that help would look like or even when it would manifest.

Leaving the water's edge, I turned back up the main street toward home. Christmas filled the tiny downtown shops with people who could afford not only food for themselves, but presents for others. As if my circumstances were not depressing enough, watching all the shoppers happily spending money only agitated me further. There would be no Christmas for me that year. I hovered dangerously near to the cliff of despair and tried to keep my footing by turning back to the bedrock of hope. I whispered, "Lord, I need to see Your miraculous provision."

Eventually, I wandered back up the street toward my apartment, located above a flower and gift shop. The window display on the first floor sparkled with life and joy, candles and flowers. The owners had gone all out. Even a Christmas tree glittered inside, beckoning customers to step into a holiday wonderland. I could only stop and look from the outside, an outsider window shopping, wishing and longing for just a little bit of that light to follow me upstairs and fill my gloomy place with joy.

My search for loose change that morning revealed that possibly I could buy that fifty-cent, bright red votive candle I stared at in the window. But then again, I could purchase a bagel. I was so discouraged that I thought I would rather buy the candle than eat. I would rather light a candle, a metaphor for kindling hope. After a few seconds of staring in the window, I decided not to buy the candle and opted to just go upstairs and save the change.

I had to do something to pull myself out of the funk and begin looking up, so I paced the apartment and spontaneously recited aloud what I knew to be true—despite evidence to the contrary.

*God will surely never leave me or forsake me*, I stated as firmly as I could while I wandered slightly dazed through the apartment, feeling beyond prayer, searching for some shred of hope to hold onto. *He promises that we would never beg for bread, but that He would provide*, I added to my weak declarations.

As I spoke up, hope washed over my soul. I knew I was lingering at the edge of the gap between the promise of the Word and the provision made manifest. Somehow, I knew His provision was close at hand and the gap was closing. Call it a momentary gift of faith or the radical foolishness of youth, but I sensed that the time for God to act was near. And so I paced and prayed.

After a few minutes, I realized that I had reached the kitchen and was standing by the refrigerator. I opened it. Still nothing inside. So I stood wishing now, not praying. "It would be so nice to have a little bag of oranges. There is something so wonderful about fresh oranges in winter." I whispered my desires to the empty room. "How nice it would be to have a loaf of fresh sourdough bread and real butter, fresh ground coffee and real cream. I don't really need steak, but some eggs would be nice, and some fresh salad even better."

The empty room absorbed my whispers, and not even the faint echo of my own voice answered back. I was truly alone, very hungry and very sad that I was helpless to finish my degree in the face of my terrible financial state. No longer whispering or declaring or praying, I fell onto my couch and started thinking about the university situation. I had come so far on my own, yet my goals still looked so far away. Perhaps in a year, I could save enough money to finish the process. Meanwhile, life stunk and I was too bewildered to create a plan. I decided to call a friend and invite myself over for dinner. But when I picked up the phone, it was dead. As I stood holding the phone, I realized I had not paid the phone bill. I was not doing a very good job of managing my life. But then again, God was supposed to meet us in our hour of need.

"Hey, God, this is my hour of need," I whispered. "Are You listening?"

Suddenly, I heard a knock at the door. I put the worthless phone down and moved to answer the door. Just as I reached out my hand to turn the doorknob, I sensed that God was indeed listening. I opened the door to the first of a series of miracles that would unfold—miracles I must receive since I knew I could not manufacture them on my own.

A girlfriend from church stood holding a bag of groceries in her hand, a sly smile turning up the corners of her face. "Hi! Merry Christmas! I was just at the grocery store and knew that you were going through a hard time, so I asked God what I should buy you."

Walking to my kitchen counter, she placed the bag on the table. A little startled, I followed her, and as she stepped aside, I reached into the bag and pulled out the contents one by one. My eyes filled with tears as I noticed not so much the objects in my hands, but the overwhelming feeling of being loved by God, who proved to me that He had heard my whispered thoughts and prayers—even before I thought them. Inside the bag was every whispered wish, purchased before I even prayed. I pulled out the bag of oranges, the sourdough bread and butter, the coffee and cream, the eggs, the makings for salad and even a couple of steaks. He provided for every little wish extravagantly.

"Oh," my friend suddenly said, glancing around at the sparsely decorated apartment and pulling out something else. "As I looked into the window of the flower shop downstairs, I saw this little red candle and thought it would add a little Christmas cheer to your apartment."

What does a woman do when faced by such love? I did what all women do—I cried. And I told my friend how God had turned her moment of listening to Him into provision beyond my wildest dreams. In the process, I realized that I had just learned a major secret to experiencing God's miraculous provision. The secret is this: Once we learn to *believe* that

God is good, a refuge in times of trouble, and that He cares for those who trust in Him, every day is Christmas. He cares about the little whispered prayers, our unspoken thoughts and wishes and dreams, He hears and He acts on our behalf . . . in His timing. We need only trust that He is good and believe that He cares.

---

## Promise

*The LORD is good,*
*a refuge in times of trouble.*
*He cares for those who trust in him.*

Nahum 1:7

---

My parents raised me to be self-reliant and independent, not interdependent. As depression-era babies, the message my parents received was, "You are on your own. Sink or swim." Coupled to that sense of survival and salvation coming from one's self, my mother's father continually tripped over his own pride and would rather that his family go hungry than accept charity. Someone would leave food or clothes outside the door of my mother's house, and her father would angrily toss it away. His six children scrounged for every penny they could earn, pilfered any scrap they could find. Life was hard, and their salvation depended on their ability to fend for themselves. They often went hungry. By the age of twelve, my mother was working a full-time job, determined to make it on her own. From the time I was a teenager, the message I received from her was, "Don't ask us for a thing. You are on your own." The feeling that left me with was that no one really cared enough about my needs and wishes and dreams to help me. So I never asked for anything.

My parents reinforced that message through their own financial struggles during the recession of the 1970s. They simply could not assist me with getting a college education, supportive though they were. Even when they had the funds, they encouraged me to work out the salvation of my financial difficulty with my own sweat. I learned not to ask for help, and I tended not to accept any offers of help from others.

The knock on the door that day when I had not a scrap of food in the house was like a knock on the door of a generational curse of pride that needed to crack wide open and reveal to me the truth about receiving from others in my community. The truth is this—learning to receive from others is, in fact, an experience in receiving gifts from the Lord. "The LORD is gracious and righteous; our God is full of compassion" (Psalm 116:5). His compassion works through others. Their hands are an extension of God's heart—our God who is gracious, generous and kind, who longs to shower gifts on His children and sees every day as Christmas.

God longs to give to a heart open to receive. The kindness of the Lord tunes in to your whispered prayers and whispers in return, *Just receive My gifts. I picked them out just for you.* The graciousness and compassion of the Lord rushes to meet our every need—not always in our timing, but always just in time. And as we tune in to His miraculous provision and receive it any way that it comes to us, we realize that the words of the psalmist in Psalm 37:25 are true: "I was young and now I am old, yet I have never seen the righteous forsaken or their children begging bread." I have never begged for bread. God has always provided that and more as I have learned to receive. He sent a knock at the door to deliver everything on my wish list that day so long ago. Not long afterward, He provided the funds I needed to repay the student loan, paid my tuition in advance and provided a free place for me to stay so that I could finish my degree in record time.

God released His generosity to me through the lives of others who were tuned in to being used as His ambassadors of love. However, lest you think that God needs people to shower you with gifts, let me tell you He is more than able to part the sea, rain down manna from heaven, stretch out His hand to heal you in the middle of the night and send His provision directly from heaven to earth—using messengers who are angels, not men.

God is able to provide abundantly, extravagantly, blowing away even the best we could imagine. Imagine desiring to give an extravagant gift to your beloved, yet having nothing in the bank to purchase it with. You know that God could provide what you need, but could He provide what you want? Then imagine the sudden appearance of a gift from heaven . . . one amazing gift that causes everything you believe about God's provision to explode into dust.

That is what happened to a young man named David Causer, a financially broke, 21-year-old newlywed with a 19-year-old wife. David desired to buy a wonderful Christmas present for Taylor, his new bride, but he had absolutely nothing to purchase it with but a wish whispered to heaven.

The couple had just moved away from their families in Tennessee to attend a ministry school in Redding, California. As often happens with ministry students, they lived on a rigidly strict budget. It was their first Christmas together as a married couple. David longed to buy his wife some wonderful token of his love, some jewelry perhaps, some gemstone. But he could not afford it. They had considered launching a ministry called "Miraculous Love" and were waiting for confirmation. If they had any extra funds, those would go into the ministry.

David asked the Lord for a way to give his wife something wonderful, something beyond the small gift he had already bought, wrapped and tucked away. He knew God would provide for their needs, but he had no idea that God wanted to provide for the longing of his heart as well. His whispered prayers and thoughts touched the heart of God. And God's response became a testimony of His miraculous love and a reflection of theirs.

David's wife, Taylor, tells the story:

David and I celebrated our first married Christmas together here in Redding before we were to leave to go home for the holidays. The day we celebrated, I had to work till evening, while David was at home. He was very sad that day because he knew we had to stick to our budget and he wasn't able to get much for me. So he went to the Lord in prayer and just started questioning if he had made the right decision in coming out to Redding for schooling or if he should have stayed home and made more money doing something else.

The Lord immediately showed him that it wasn't things material I wanted; it was just his love and being with him that I wanted. When I got home, we exchanged gifts and celebrated Jesus! It was truly the best Christmas I have ever had!

As we were going to bed, we pulled back our covers, and David spotted a glittery thing in the center. He reached down to grab it and throw it out, but as he held it, he realized it was not just glitter or shiny paper; it was a diamond from heaven. The Lord gave us a Christmas gift worth far more than anything we could have given each other. Our hearts were filled suddenly with joy and crazy love for our Daddy!

The very next day, I was sharing with some friends at school about it, and one of the girls said it reminded her of the Scripture in Hebrews 13 that says the bed of the married should be holy. And I thought to myself, *Well, kind of but not really, because that verse talks about adultery.* But we looked it up anyway, and the very next verse after that one said, "Keep your life free from the love of money, and be content with what you have, for He has said, 'I will never leave you nor forsake you.'"

*Wow!* What a word from the Lord! So basically, God just wanted to remind us that money should not be an issue. He has us in His hands and knows what we need and what we want. He owns the universe, including diamonds!

After Taylor related her story to me, David added that he immediately noticed the diamond was an exact replica of the diamond in Taylor's wedding ring, so he reached for Taylor's hand to see if the stone had fallen out. It was still set securely in her ring. What was this strange miracle? Where had the diamond come from? Later on, when he took it in for an appraisal, the jeweler offered to purchase it on the spot—for $10,000. The diamond was real.

As David and Taylor pondered the mystery, the meaning unfolded. They realized that their marriage bed was holy in the sense that the unity in their marriage was sanctified, set apart as a testimony to God's miraculous love. For David, the appearance of a diamond also revealed the confirmation they needed to launch the ministry under the name "Miraculous Love."[1] The diamond's sudden appearance released the awareness to them that God was more than able to provide extravagantly; that God, in fact, knew the thoughts and desires of David's heart and provided miraculously, lavishly, beyond his ability to imagine.

The diamond was a token of love and a miracle of provision. And it almost got swept away, off the bed, onto the carpet for the vacuum cleaner to suck into oblivion. Pay attention to the little things that drop into your life and receive them with awe and wonder. They may just be God's miraculous provision for you . . . for now and perhaps for someday in the future.

> Pay attention to the little things that drop into your life and receive them with awe and wonder. They may just be God's miraculous provision for you . . . for now and perhaps for someday in the future.

The Causers' story reminded me of another young couple on a journey, a couple who were also newlyweds. Already pregnant, she was ready to give birth. Little did they know that they would not be able to return home for a couple of years. They had not provisioned for such a long journey. How would they survive? The gifts of three wise men—gold, frankincense and myrrh—provisioned them for the journey and enabled them to live more easily during their sojourn in a foreign land. They were birthday gifts for their newborn son, and more importantly, tokens of love from a Father in heaven who knew their anxious thoughts and heard their whispered prayers. This loving Father had already provided for them months before they were to experience the moment of their greatest need. Long before, He had moved the hearts of men to saddle up and ride out in search of the newborn baby King . . . a child who had not been born when they began their journey to present Him with their gifts.

Every day is Christmas. Every day, God provides for us in some miraculous way that may seem mundane or a product of our own routine. We need to stop and pay attention to the little objects glittering in our path and receive the gifts of God, no matter how small they seem. The secret to receiving more of God's provision begins with tuning in to the possibility of a miracle presenting itself every day. Watch for it. Wait for it. And receive it when it comes.

Those who tune in to the possibility of miracles generally stand poised to recognize them and receive them—big or small, material or spiritual. God is generous and longs to interact with us every single day.

May the Lord now show you kindness and faithfulness and release to you the knowledge that we, His children, will never beg for bread, never be forsaken and always be heard. He hears our whispers, and He delights in releasing His miraculous provision . . . not a stingy provision, but a lavish expression of His love, personally expressed.

# 2

## LIVING ON THE CURRENCY OF GOD'S LOVE

We all live with some undercurrent of fear shaping the course of our lives. I have lived so frugally all of my life that I never stepped out to make a big purchase—like a top-of-the-line car or even my own home. I lived with the mindset that I was poor, and wealth was not something that I strove for or desired, although I always wanted a more settled life in my own home rather than renting a succession of apartments or houses, as I had been doing. One day while spending the weekend in a little cottage on Eagles Nest Farm, which is owned by a wonderful older couple named Paul and Gretel Haglin near St. Louis, I went for a long walk in the woods. As I walked, I took up the matter with the Lord.

"Lord, what is it that hinders me from prospering?" I asked.

I started thinking about my plans for the future and the next steps in my life and wondered if I should step out and buy a house. The whole nation seemed to be sliding into the grip of a long recession, and foreclosures were beginning to decimate families and communities. It seemed like the right time for me to buy, but I feared being able to make future payments on the mortgage. What if something happened to my job? Or my health? After all, I am a single woman. If something happened to me, I had no one to rescue me.

Suddenly, I sensed the Lord say, *Stop here, on the path, and drive a stick named fear in the ground and declare that it will no longer have a hold on your life.* So I picked up a stick and drove it into the soggy, springtime ground and stood for a moment staring at it. Then the Lord said, *Take another stick and drive it into the ground and declare that poverty will no longer have a hold on your life.* So I took another stick and drove it into the ground a couple feet away from the first stick, stood back and stared at it. The two sticks looked like a little gate on a county road.

Suddenly, the air in the middle of the gate and above the gate started shimmering like a heat wave dancing above hot asphalt. That shimmering usually indicates the presence of an angel. And I felt its presence. Then the shimmering opened like a door to the other side, and I saw that the gate led to another dimension of heaven on earth. I walked through the gate, lifting my arms up in worship, declaring the goodness of God and declaring that fear and poverty would no longer have a hold on me. Then, to my surprise, I found myself forcefully stating, "I am a prosperous soul! I will prosper without fear of the future!"

As I passed through the gate, the open vision of walking through the gate of heaven ended. I felt completely different. I felt as though I had entered into a new dimension of heaven that has been released for me to walk in on earth—a dimension of trust, of lasting favor and peace and joy; a place where there is no residual fear of poverty, or of not being able to pay the mortgage or my bills. Trust in Abba's faithfulness was all that remained! Perhaps what was imparted during this spiritual experience was a deep gift of trust and a sense of security. Fear of the future flees when you are swept into God's embrace and declare the promise of God over your life.

## The Currency of God's Love

Being reduced to living on the currency of God's love positions you to move from ordinary provision to extraordinary prosperity. God has not given you a spirit of fear, but of love, joy, peace and a sound mind (see 2 Timothy 1:7). His promise is that as a child of the King of kings, you have a right to His inheritance on earth as it is in heaven. A friend of mine whose story is just ahead had to learn that she was not stupid. Rather, God saw her as His delight, the apple of His eye, her worth far beyond her own estimation of her value. His love cast out her fear and emboldened her to reach out and love others. Her finances changed. She entered into her calling and stepped into her destiny. And as she came into alignment with her destiny, doors of prosperity opened to her. But it all began with encountering God's love.

I stepped into a gift of faith once I declared that fear and poverty would no longer have a hold on me. I also entered into a new covenant with the Lord. As I broke covenant with the mindset of poverty, I entered into the covenant of prospering. But that prosperity is conditional.

Prosperity depends on knowing God's love and trusting in it every day—despite evidence to the contrary. We often live in the gap between the promise of provision and actually seeing the miracle we need come to pass before our eyes. How many times have you cried out to God for something you needed right then and there? Every day, people petition for dire needs. "God, heal me." "God, save my marriage." "God, will You pay the rent? I need funds to pay the electric bill, the heating bill, the mortgage." "God! Help!"

His ear is not deaf to your need. Neither is His arm too short to stretch out from heaven and rearrange things on earth to save you (see Isaiah 59:1). But as we peer across the wide and vacant expanse between our need and God's provision, we can stumble into the abyss of despair. Trusting in His love keeps us from falling over the edge.

## Connect to God's Love

The most challenging question that hits all of us in desperate times seems to be this: How do we live without the inner turmoil of fear when all seems lost? How do we rest, our hearts at peace, in the gap between hearing and reading God's promises of provision and seeing the reality of that provision manifesting? When we stand empty-handed and grief stricken, beyond our own ability to provide, what is the secret to sustaining faith and hope as we peer into the vast gap between promise and provision?

We also find this same principle when the apostle John prayed, "Dear friend, I pray that you may enjoy good health and that all may go well with you, even as your soul is getting along well" (3 John 2). "That all may go well with you" is also translated as "prosper." The Greek word for "prosper" comes from the prefix *eu*, which means "to be happy," and from the root word *odos*, "a way or path, also a journey." So to prosper literally means to find happiness in your journey. It can also mean to succeed in reaching your goal. It appears John is saying that God desires for every area of your life to prosper.

God desires that you prosper in your soul, and it begins with connecting to the love that God has for you. When your soul prospers, then your mind is being transformed. You should see a reflection of prosperity transforming all the affairs of your life, making you whole. Being prosperous includes everything you do, think and believe. It means you should be making

40

progress in reaching toward the prize of your high calling in Christ Jesus. Your health, finances, marriage, business and ministry should prosper. Your whole life should reflect the prosperity of your soul. If your soul is depleted, your life will be depleted.

I believe that the greatest need in every human on earth is the need for love—pure, unconditional love filling you until your heart sings with joy. And when you start singing out of the abundance of God's love filling you, you go forth into the world lighter, brighter and more attractive to others.

Knowing God's love is the beginning of true prosperity.

You begin to attract the favor of God and man when you walk around with a smile on your face, the evidence of God's love radiating from you. Knowing God's love is the beginning of true prosperity.

## Walking through the Gate of Love

A friend of mine discovered this love one day. When God's love suddenly walked into her life, it ushered her into a season of visions that unlocked her heart to know Jesus more intimately than she ever dreamed. And as her soul prospered under the nurturing care of Jesus' loving presence, she began to prosper in other areas of her life. Her name will remain confidential to protect the privacy of those involved, but here is her account of being ambushed by love one night. She had been called forward to speak to the church about how God's power met her during a conference she had attended. Much to her amazement, she found her testimony cut short as she was ambushed by the power of God once again. She describes what happened:

> Have you ever tried to move a part of your body, and it wouldn't move? Maybe hitting your funny bone, and your

hand wouldn't move? Well, I could not get up. I was glued to the ground. After trying several times to push myself up, I gave up and just thought I would stay lying down and listen to the rest of the service. But God had another idea . . .

I looked up. I saw the brightest, most beautiful light. I was in awe at the beauty. I kept saying to my friend nearby, "Look! It's so beautiful." The "light" kept coming closer and growing. I don't understand how, but I knew it was God's glory, His very presence.

The glory got so low that I could reach my hand out and touch it. Oh, how soft it was, how smooth, how wonderful it was. It kept coming down and became so bright that I could barely keep my eyes open. I kept putting my hand over my eyes, peeking through my fingers until I had to keep my eyes shut or be blinded—and still it kept coming. Every breath I took, I would breathe it in. It filled my lungs and permeated my very being. It was heavy and was pushing me down, even though I was on the floor.

Then I knew that I couldn't take this glory on my physical being anymore. I knew I was going to die. I wasn't afraid; I didn't care. What a way to go. I very calmly told Him, "Well, I'm going to die now," and I waited in His presence . . . but it started to withdraw. I didn't realize it at first. I could open my eyes and see it again; I could wave my hand through it again. That's when I realized it was receding. I called out to Him, "Don't go, or if You go, take me with You!" I didn't want to live without that presence.

Within this presence, His glory, resided a love that was incomprehensible; love that even went beyond 1 Corinthians 13 love, the love that Paul prays we would know, the love of Christ, which surpasses knowledge. Surpasses . . . to go beyond what was expected or hoped for, usually by being bigger, better or greater. This love was beyond my expectation; it was beyond what I could ever have imagined and, therefore, ever hoped for. It was bigger and better and greater than anything I could ever have thought possible. I knew this love was His love for me . . . for you . . . for everyone. No matter how evil they were, He still loved them. It was for the drug addict, the murderer, the terrorist.

His love was complete. He doesn't love one over the other. His heart beats with love. He truly is love. I know . . . I felt it, saw it, breathed it.

And now I have to digress. You see, this was the first time in my life I had felt love. I thought I was someone who just couldn't be loved. Silly thought, maybe, but the circumstances in my life told me it was true.

My dad didn't want me. While other children went by cute little nicknames, my nickname was hurtful, meant to show how stupid my dad thought I was. If I spilled my milk at dinner (which I must admit was often), my dinner was put on the kitchen floor and I was told I had to eat like a dog because I was sloppy, or I was put in the bathtub with my food. I also had a brother whom my dad seemed to like a lot. Whenever my dad would have to take us somewhere, he would tell my brother to come with him and tell me to stay in the car. He was ashamed of me, and I didn't understand why.

It became clear when I was in the first grade that I wasn't as bright as the other children, but it wasn't until I was in the eighth grade that I was tested and found to have learning disabilities. I was then put in what was at the time called the mentally retarded class. Maybe this was why my dad was ashamed of me.

I wrote Dear Abby once when I was about nine years old and asked her why my dad hated me so much, though I tried to do what was right. The letter was never sent. My mother gave it to my dad. I can remember sitting on the end of my bed, right by my door, and listening. I was hoping my dad would say he did love me, but instead, he bellowed that maybe he could love me if I wasn't so stupid. Ahhh, now I knew: I was stupid. You must not be able to love a stupid person.

But, you may ask, what about the love of my mother? When I was three or four years old, my mother had been painting the living room. She had left a cup of paint thinner, turpentine, on the kitchen table. I awoke from a nap and went into the kitchen. Thinking the cup was filled with water, I drank it. I was rushed to the hospital and had my stomach pumped. I almost died a few days later when my kidneys started to shut down. I found out much later that my mother called a doctor and begged him to come to the house. We didn't have much money, and she told him she would pay him a dollar a month for the rest of her life. He had compassion, came to the house and put me on antibiotics, and again my life was saved. Maybe I could have talked to my mother when I was older, but by then she was a full-fledged alcoholic and physically, mentally and emotionally wasn't there for anyone.

My dad's mother came to live with us shortly after that. I found out later that my grandmother didn't like my mother and tried to talk my dad into leaving her. One day when my grandmother was taking care of my brother and me, she took me on her lap and told me that my mother had left the paint thinner down on purpose because I was no good. She said that I would never be any good no matter how hard I tried, because my mother was evil.

After I was married, my grandmother was dying of cancer and kept asking for me. She was so emaciated that she didn't even look like herself. My dad and his sister didn't tell me she wanted to see me because they didn't want me to see her like that. Out of four grandchildren, I was the only one she was asking for. She became so insistent about seeing me that the family finally relented and had me come. By the time I got there, she was in a coma and was unable to communicate. When she had realized she was dying, she had asked forgiveness from my mother and all those whom she had hurt. She was then ready to go, except for one thing. I believe the reason she so desperately wanted to see me was because she wanted to ask my forgiveness also, but it was too late.

Everyone does things that they think are stupid, and they usually get over them. But every time I did something stupid, I was told that was why I couldn't be loved. It was a constant reminder to me: Stupid equals unlovable.

I married, but never believed my husband loved me. I still did stupid things. I had children, but I knew as soon as

44

they were old enough and saw that I did stupid things, they, too, wouldn't love me. Oh, but how I loved them.

I believe that one of the things the enemy does is try to keep us silent. I was embarrassed and ashamed, so I never talked about it. I became quiet and withdrawn. I didn't like talking to people because then they would find out how stupid I was. I lived in a world filled with fear of discovery. I learned to hide. I don't think anyone who knew me knew how I felt or what I went through. I was silent and hurt.

So when I felt, saw, breathed God's love into my life, it literally changed my life. Someone loved me. I was amazed. I feel so in love with this God who loved me. At that moment I gained a Father, Brother, Teacher, Companion and Friend, not someone I read about, but Someone I knew and not only knew, but who knew me and loved me. Loved me with an incomprehensible love that I experienced. I was convinced that neither death, nor life, nor angels, nor principalities, nor things present, nor things to come, nor powers, nor height, nor depth, nor any other created thing, would be able to separate me from the love of God, which is in Christ Jesus my Lord.

As my friend learned to rest in the presence of the God who revealed His love to her and continues to reveal His love every day, her life changed. God transformed her from a fearful and silent woman into a key intercessor with a ministry of her own. Love released her fear, healed her soul and launched her into a ministry that is thriving and gaining worldwide attention.

## Letting Go of Fear and Poverty

When someone encounters the sudden love of God breaking into their world, two main hindrances to prosperity shatter. Those hindrances are fear and poverty. Perfect love, or the experience of encountering perfect love, casts out fear. "There is no fear in love; but perfect love casts out fear, because

fear involves punishment, and the one who fears is not per-
fected in love" (1 John 4:18, NASB). God's Word gives us this
guarantee:

---

## *Promise*

*Love will release you from fear.*

---

When you are released from the fear of failure or fear
of success, the paralyzing fear of lack of money to meet
upcoming bills, the impending doom of bankruptcy, fear of
relationships crumbling, fear of the future and the host of
newscasts that breed fear of disease and disaster, you have
much more energy available to prosper. It is a prosperity fu-
eled by a divine encounter and by joy.

If you want to prosper, first your soul must prosper. Souls
prosper as they step into an encounter with God's love. That's
the first important key to unlocking prosperity. Seek after it. I
have seen people in extreme financial poverty who lived joyfully
on the currency of knowing God's love. Love was all they had to
feast on when meals trickled down to two or three a week—not
a day. Knowing and trusting in God's love sustained them.

### Living in the Gap

Ruthless trust in Abba's ability to hear and to act is the second
important key to unlocking prosperity. God loves you and
will provide for you beyond your wildest dreams, although
not in ways that you expect. God sovereignly dispenses the
miraculous in different ways. Sometimes acting alone, He
moves heaven to respond. Other times, He moves a person
to respond and meet the need in someone else's life.

Living in that in-between state—the gap—between the
unanswered prayer requests and the manifestation of provi-

sion demands that we take a big breath of His love and exhale trust, ruthless trust. The secret to living in that gap between promise and provision is understanding this: "Godliness with contentment is great gain" (1 Timothy 6:6). Godliness, to me, means dwelling in God's love, close to the heart of the Father, becoming one with Him. It means steadying my anxious thoughts by choosing to trust that though I do not see His provision, He will come through.

Godliness focuses on Him as the provider rather than blaming Him as the instigator of your woes and blows. Do not compare your prosperity to another's prosperity. I know that is not easy when the sky is falling, the mortgage is months overdue, your sister or brother seems more prosperous than you, you feel ashamed and afraid, you just got fired from your job or your spouse just walked out with everything you had in your emotional and financial bank accounts. Godliness, dwelling in His love and in His grace, will enable you to be at peace, content with what you have. Living on the currency of God's love lifts you to a higher level of contentment, one that cannot be shaken by materialistic downturns or perceived shortcomings.

*Living in that in-between state—the gap—between the unanswered prayer requests and the manifestation of provision demands that we take a big breath of His love and exhale trust, ruthless trust.*

When you make comparisons, envy and covetousness are the results that spin you into a pit of despair. When you choose to enter into contentment with what you have today, thanksgiving takes root and blossoms into peace. Focus on Jesus—Jehovah Jirah, our provider—thank Him for the soon-to-come unveiling of His thoughts and ways. But beware—His provision may not look like what you want because God has destined for us to live in an alternate Kingdom—His Kingdom based on a currency of love. Learning to live on that love and ruthlessly trusting Him will see you through to the end!

## Rich Sister/Poor Sister

It is not all that easy to be content with what you have. Quite often, I have turned to Psalm 73 and let God's Word steer my thoughts back to God's grace that reduces us to living large on the currency of love. God's grace enables us to find contentment in the midst of chaos.

Attempting to boost myself up into loftier mindsets about prosperity, I will often wander into the local bookstore and pull business books off the shelves. One book caught my attention with its provocative title—*Rich Dad, Poor Dad* by Robert Kiyosaki (Business Plus, 2000). Immediately, the title caused me to remember the story of two sisters who were friends of mine. One was a Christian, and the other was quite caught up in the materialistic aspirations of contemporary American culture. Here is their story:

> While Annie always seemed to prosper, Sandra felt for years that she received only the bare necessities of God's provision. At times, Sandra watched her sister with a heart full of envy. Annie graduated from college with a marriage proposal in hand from a really good, Christian man. By the time Sandra graduated from college, her college boyfriend had moved away to launch his career, and she took the first job she could find—a low-paying social work position.
>
> Annie and her husband both worked, and they planned out their lives in such a way that they did not seem to need faith in God to get by. They thought they were doing fine on their own, and she was fast becoming the rich sister. For a while, they lived in a beautiful house and started their family.

When their second child was due, Annie's husband accepted a job promotion, and they moved to an even more luxurious neighborhood. They were living the American dream—a house, two children, a dog, two cars, lots of friends and parties to attend.

Sandra, however, focused on saving the world and ministering to the lost, the poor and the broken. Not much money in that line of work, but she justified it by believing that she was laying up treasure in heaven. She was young and had time to burn. She gave no thought to saving for old age, which seemed so far away. Throughout the years, Sandra learned to trust in God's love, and time after time she saw His ability to provide. Her heart nestled securely in His arms of love, and she focused on being with Him and ministering to others rather than furthering her career to elevate her financial status. Sandra lived in rental houses, while her rich sister lived in her own home. Sandra spent her money on overseas missions and urban ministry, investing it in the Kingdom, laying up treasure in heaven. Annie spent money on trips to Hawaii and skied all winter long until she began having children.

Because both sisters grew up in a secular home, Sandra was considered the black sheep of the family—the Christian sister who often used her funds for missions rather than for gaining material possessions, the one who chose to minister to others and missed out on a conventional life. Sandra was the poor sister in her family's eyes and in the eyes of many others. Extended family members, some of them wealthy evangelicals, considered her foolish for not living up to her income potential, for failing to marry well and buy a house or two. In their eyes, Sandra was barely hanging on to God's provision and was far from gaining wealth. After all, wealth and comfort are what prosperity means, right?

Everything the rich sister and her husband touched turned to gold. Sandra brushed aside her envy and tried to be content with what she had. Eventually, she realized that when she compared herself to her rich sister or to her prosperous friends, she became depressed. *There has to be a middle ground of serving God and being comfortable this side of heaven,* she often thought. Although she loved serving God, secretly Sandra also thought, *Annie is really the one who has it all.*

But then one day, Annie's perfect husband—who liked his evening cocktails and his idealism of the high life—touched the wrong thing, and their lives quickly unraveled. After they separated, the rich sister moved into a poor neighborhood. Her troubles melted Sandra's heart. The poor sister had always known that life was not as happy as it seemed for Annie, and her envy subsided every time she prayed for Annie and her family. Bankruptcy followed divorce, and eventually Annie became caught up in the mortgage crisis of 2007–2008. The rich sister was becoming the poor sister, caught up in the struggle for her life and for her children's futures.

Meanwhile, the poor one was now in a position to acquire property, and her income continued to increase substantially every year. Sandra was learning to prosper financially during this season in her life, while Annie was learning a lesson her sister was already very familiar with—how to trust in God and rest contentedly in His ability to provide—no matter what that provision looked like. Annie's children, too, entered into a season of learning about a whole new set of values based on love rather than money.

During this economic downturn, the sisters gathered at their parents' house to celebrate Annie's birthday. They stretched out to watch the depression-era movie *Kit Kittredge.* Annie's eight-year-old daughter and ten-year-old son snuggled in on both sides of her as they watched one family in the movie lose their house. The bank's representatives carried off the kids' toys and furniture, while the mother and daughter stood by, helplessly crying. Some stern-looking man hammered a foreclosure sign into the lawn, and as the camera refocused on Kit and her friends, one youngster asked, "Where will they go?"

The movie soon revealed where newly pauperized neighbors went—to a relative's house, a boardinghouse or a shelter of some sort. Fathers left to find work in other cities. Hobo camps along the river overflowed with the former middle class and the poor alike. Soup kitchens kept people from starving. Eventually, fathers returned to their homes and prosperity blossomed once again. As usual, a story filled with pain, drama and a little mystery had a Hollywood happy ending. The main point, though, seemed to be that love is the true prosperity, the currency of a value system that transcends this world.

While the credits rolled up the screen, Annie's little girl spoke up a bit anxiously. "That doesn't happen anymore, does it?" she asked. "People aren't losing their houses like that, are they?"

Her optimistic and protective older brother immediately replied, "Daddy's working. He's got a good job. It couldn't happen to us."

Their childlike faith in Daddy's ability to provide for them and shield them from life's economic blows brought peace to them that night. And as Annie and Sandra talked about the movie with the children, they all agreed that being loved was better than being rich, and having each other was more important than having stuff.

Little did Annie's kids know that their parents' assets had long ago been severed in the divorce. Daddy's economic security did not necessarily transfer to their mother. Their mother had moved quickly in the aftermath of the shock of losing her husband to another woman. She secured an interest-only loan and moved into the cheapest house she could find during the high point of the housing market. Now she owned a worthless house in a rapidly declining area. Gangs were taking over the neighborhood. It was time to leave. Her only option was to walk away from the house and let it fall into foreclosure.

The children were oblivious to their mother's plans. Daddy did not live too far away, and the children had established friendships in his neighborhood. Their mom had even started them in after-school sports teams in Daddy's neighborhood rather than keeping them on the teams in their own area. At the end of the foreclosure process, all these children would know is that they had moved to a safer neighborhood, closer to Daddy's house. They would rent a house. Eventually, their mom might buy another one, in time.

Transitions do not have to be traumatic. God is more than able to take our decisions and reactions and weave them into a greater design for prosperity than we can imagine. His value system and Kingdom are not of this world. God's grace provides peace in the midst of the storm, shields us like children, releases strategy and finances for us to move on, imparts grace to enter into His value system and opens our hearts to a higher love in the process. Our part to play in this Kingdom is to let go of our own plans and fall into the arms of the Creator of the world. He is more than able to care for us and even prosper us. We need to learn to live in the experience of His grace, which provides for our every step in the journey of life.

One day, Sandra told me that Annie had called and said, "I know that you've prayed for angels to protect the house, and I feel their presence. I know that angels are surrounding my house because the neighborhood's troubles and the gangs haven't touched us." On another day, Annie called and said that she had started praying again and feeling more peace. Sandra could tell that in the midst of the foreclosure process, Annie's heart was reawakening to God's love. One day Annie simply told Sandra that losing the house was preferable to being unable to keep her family safe and together. Annie was being reduced to love.

God's love was Annie's provision during this season. His grace enabled her to bridge the gap between the promise of His provision and the reality of its manifestation, which looked so different from what she had expected. And both sisters realized that God's love is the great keeping force on earth—keeping us safe, providing what we need no matter the circumstances, keeping His eye on us and sending His angels to keep watch over us. God releases strategy during difficult times so that we can prosper and redirects us so our hearts grow rich in peace as we become even more aware of His ever-present love.

## True Prosperity

Experiencing Kingdom prosperity in every area of your life and in every season of your life means that you must keep your heart open and be reduced to love . . . not provoked to envy or coveting what others have. Beauty and riches in this world fade away quickly. Envy locks you into a poverty mentality and makes it difficult to break out and prosper in ways that you desire. But we have an unshakable Kingdom we live in as Christians, a Kingdom based on an extraordinarily loving God who calls us to live in His love and give it away. Both tangibles and intangibles reveal the measure of prosperity you live in. True prosperity involves having enough to give away—both enough love and enough material goods.

True prosperity begins with your soul prospering in love. True prosperity comes when you realize that holding onto your family is more valuable than holding onto a house. It comes when seeing yourself reflected in the loving eyes of God is more valuable than seeking wealth and looking good in the eyes of the world. It comes when seeking after a higher love and the exquisite joy you feel as His presence sweeps you off your feet is more valuable than chasing after clandestine affairs. The Kingdom of God releases the true prosperity of righteousness, peace and joy, which flood your soul until you join your thoughts with His thoughts, your value system with His. And having learned to live in God's love, you find that envy fades away, your soul

> True prosperity involves having enough to give away—both enough love and enough material goods.

prospers and now you are positioned to prosper in other, more tangible ways.

While the rich sister learned about God's love and entered into a new value system, the poor sister started learning to prosper materially. The economy ruins some people; homes tumble into foreclosures and people lose their jobs. Yet other people like the poor sister, who had learned to live on the Kingdom-based currency of love, stood positioned to prosper materially and be entrusted with more. As those in the world who had overextended themselves financially faced the repercussions of an economic downturn, many others were suddenly looking wise for not living beyond their means. The Fed lowered the interest rates on mortgages to a record low, and suddenly the poor sister could afford a home, while the rich sister was losing hers. But both now knew that whatever their circumstances, their true prosperity began with God's love.

My own meager savings at that time also enabled me to purchase a property and jump when I heard God say, "Act now." And so, after that long walk in the woods where I declared that fear and poverty would no longer have a hold on my mind, I was free to act on the opportunity to step into home ownership. I acted. But I still live on the currency of love and ruthless trust. I always will.

During the years that I had to learn to live in the gap between promise and provision, resting in God's grace and struggling past envy and into contentment, I was living on the currency of love. I had to learn to see with new eyes what true prosperity is. I needed to learn how to live graciously in the gap between the promise of His provision and receiving His provision—without falling into the pit of despair or envy or greed and stepping outside God's will and value system to provide for myself. Now what I gain materially is no more to me than a mere tangible expression of the currency of love that I get to give away.

Spiritually, prosperity is receiving God's miraculous provision every day, often in unexpected ways. Scripture reveals a long history of God's miraculous care for His people. While Israel's twelve tribes wandered forty years in the desert, God miraculously provided food and clothing for them despite the fact that they carried hundreds of pounds of gold and silver—worthless goods in the desert, a weight, in fact, that many probably wanted to drop for the desert sands to sweep in and cover up.

In another story, Elijah walked through a period of famine and drought. Living by a stream, he was fed by ravens who took the king's food and dropped it in Elijah's lap. The raven was an unclean bird, its symbolism kind of like having demons drop food in your lap or having to endure some distasteful job under a morally repugnant boss in order to survive. But the provision was sanctified by the hand of God, and Elijah dared not turn it away. Eventually, God directed him to a widow's house and called them to live in community and experience the miraculous provision of God supplying food and maintaining the roof over their heads.

God's faithfulness revealed in Scripture causes us to know that He is the One who sees, and His provision comes always and forever. We all need to learn to live through the lean times, contented to accept God's provision—no matter how foolish or unusual it looks to others.

## Choose the Provision, Not the Problem

Both rich and poor sister in the story have learned how to choose the provision over the problem and be content with what that provision looks like in every circumstance. God will always provide a way of escape from any problem. And He will always provide wisdom and strategy when we sit and listen. Sometimes, He provides miraculously. Other times, He calls us to draw near to Him, to listen for the word that He sends, to hear and to act.

We all need to learn to live through the lean times, contented to accept God's provision— no matter how foolish or unusual it looks to others.

Choose to dwell on Jehovah Jirah, our provider. Choose to receive the provision that He sends. Focus on the One who gives grace for the journey and enlarges our faith to receive more than we could ever ask or imagine. Choose to live contented with what He provides rather than grumbling about what He is not providing. That is the secret to experiencing God's generosity and living large on the currency of love. God's provision for heartache, for poverty, for love, for healing and for joy releases more than enough for you and me to prosper and give abundantly to others. Life may be hard at times, but God is always good. One of God's names is El-Shaddai, which means "The God of More than Enough." As we think about our lives, the things we need, the things we desire and the things necessary to carry out the plans of God, remember that we worship the God of more than enough.

# 3

## ANGELS WATCHING OVER YOU

For he will command his angels concerning you
    to guard you in all your ways;
they will lift you up in their hands,
    so that you will not strike your foot against a stone.

Psalm 91:11–12

The serenity I felt, despite knowing the worst was happening, haunts me to this day. I could not imagine a more gentle moment than this surrendering to the end—it was nothing like I had conceived it would be. The end itself seemed merely a slow and gentle swim through the aqua garden of God.

First, I saw the giant green turtle resting lightly on the bottom sand just as the other divers swam away. That left a place for me to observe it alone. I prefer to swim at a distance from others, partly due to my nature—aversive to crowds—partly due to a voyeuristic tendency to stare uninterrupted at life happening in an ecosystem forcign to my own. Next, I noticed two smaller turtles swaying slightly in the surge that nudged their huge backs, gently rocking them like a mother's hand upon a cradle. No wonder they all nodded off, taking their morning nap 45 feet beneath the surface of the Hawaiian sea. I kicked my long fins for a closer look, the water offering no resistance to me despite the unpleasant necessity of a tank strapped to my back, cumbersome as a turtle's shell.

Theoretically, I could stay at this depth without incident for as long as I could breathe. My tank of compressed air still held about 35 minutes of time. Theoretically, I could observe the turtles for another half hour. At this depth, the Navy dive tables also showed that no decompression would be required before surfacing. Diver lore consistently reported that there was no risk of the euphoric effects of nitrogen narcosis that impacts some divers at depths of 80 to 120 feet. I therefore anticipated an uneventful dive, the last in a week of diving in these gentle Kona waters. With visibility of over 100 feet, I was still within sight of my fellow divers swimming away.

I dropped to my knees, eye to eye with the largest turtle, whose tiny head bobbed forward as it fought sleep to keep a wary eye on me. Yellow tang scooted across his back, cleaning his shell. Butterfly fish nipped one another playfully near his fin. I wished I had a video camera to capture the moment, my private witness to life's symbiotic playfulness. It would have been something to watch when I am an old woman remembering the days when my bones and muscles worked according to my will. I would remember the Dr. Seuss-like places they took me both tropical and alpine, the sensuous pleasures felt, scents and sounds that will serve as vague reminders of a life well lived. My mind is my only camera, though. I have years of images stored inside some neuron vault that replays surreal movies in my sleep. I know they will serve me well in my old age, when I sit rocking, chuckling at secrets that leave people shaking their heads, wondering what goes on in an old woman's mind. The image of that turtle day in the undersea garden of God will figure prominently when I am old and gray. I am certain of that.

I knelt in the sand, watching the turtle, the fish, coral-crusted lava flows, patches of white sand, plankton gliding by in the vague current. Translucent schools of stretched-out coronet fish swam, their backs pinstriped with neon streaks of turquoise sprinkled with aboriginal dots. Their button eyes watched me watching them. Damsel fish wove along, arrayed in black-and-yellow stripes, swimming a dance of the bumblebees. I laughed at the ballet *dans la mer* and imagined an accompanying symphony.

I felt at peace here, so relaxed that I knew I could lie down, curl up beside the turtle, toss an arm across his back and drift off. My eyelids felt heavy with the thought. Too heavy. I wondered at this easy descent into my imagination. Alarmed, I stood up, my fins firmly underneath me, my heels dug into the sand. The turtle startled for a moment, raised its head questioningly and then nodded off again.

Suddenly, the water swirled clockwise, spinning, my body caught up in a vertigo that made me wonder if I were spinning, too. But it was all in my head, now drifting into these clouds that had somehow descended into the sea. The swirl changed direction, and I felt myself lifting then falling, as if dancing with some chaotic partner manic in his movements, caught up in ecstasy and taking me along for his ride. I was drunk, intoxicated beyond reason, as the sparkly ocean swirled around me. I felt caught up in awe. I knew I was in trouble here, intoxicated by oxygen deprivation or nitrogen narcosis or something like it. My hand reached out for anything to steady me, keep me from falling or rising—my body lost in this atmosphere. I was spun out, yet I had not moved.

My knees buckled into the sand once more. The turtle looked alarmed. We stared eye to eye again as my head dropped down, bobbing in the current. He nodded at me as if I belonged there in the turtle napping grounds, accepted me. I am *ohana*, his family now. No doubt we felt this lovely peace together, the water caressing our faces, yellow tangs and trigger fish surely playing on the back of my tank, which felt surprisingly light—so light I felt naked but for this thing in my mouth. Although I knew it was the regulator that brought air from the tank to my lips, I could not remember why this bulky object was there and wanted to spit it out so I could talk to the turtles unencumbered. No answer marched into my mind. Words are the first to drown. Reason becomes unnecessary when you feel such a deep, deep rest.

I surrendered, intoxicated, as if 45 years of unshed weariness pressed me into the sand conspiratorially, 45 feet beneath the surface as shallow water blackout engulfed me. Slipping into unconsciousness, my eyes fought like a child resisting bedtime, blinking back darkness, focusing on the light before me shrinking in on itself. I could not rouse myself, only surrender, let go. No noise but the deep and rhythmic breathing of a detached body that I knew was mine sounded in my ears, slowing down, no demands, no worries, no fear, no past or future, a totally emotionless void now leading to oblivion. My face drifted lower, settling onto the ocean floor. I smiled. This was the way it should be; this dropping nonchalantly from one life into the next.

"Get moving!"

I heard a voice closer to me than my own heartbeat, authoritative but gentle. My brain heard it and ignored it, but my muscles responded as the unseen voice speaking those two words lifted me by the arms, dragged me backward off the sand and hurtled me toward the other divers about 100 feet away, hidden behind a wall of lava. My feet reflexively kicked twice as my body squirmed into reality. The action woke me reluctantly. Although I felt slightly groggy, reason now prevailed. I swam toward the wall just as the other divers emerged into sight, and I finished the dive swimming in the company of others. I surfaced a few minutes early and climbed over the transom of the dive boat, saying nothing on the return to Honokohau Harbor.

This blissful moment in the undersea garden of God passed without the tragedy of my demise, yet it left me incredibly aware that angels "swim." And I also know this now—that come what may, I will not fear nature's dangers, nor the plots of man, for I have this assurance:

---

## Promise

*When you pass through the waters,*
*I will be with you;*
*and when you pass through the rivers,*
*they will not sweep over you.*
*When you walk through the fire,*
*you will not be burned . . .*
*For I am the LORD, your God. . . .*
*Do not be afraid, for I am with you.*

Isaiah 43:2–3, 5

---

Yet this knowledge comes with a price—the price of living for a long while afterward haunted by the feeling of that exquisite peace flooding in when one surrenders this earthly atmosphere for eternity. It left me standing in the slack tide of my own existence, gazing longingly out to sea for the rest of that vacation. And I was left to ponder why God had sent His angel to rescue me and how best to fill the long meanwhile between now and the moment when the tide will gently come and carry me through the tall pearl gate, iridescent in beauty, opening the way into forever with the Creator-King.

For weeks afterward, I felt an anger rising during my prayer times. I felt as if I had stepped so close to heaven, only to be turned away. "Why, God, did You save me from the bottom of the sea?" I asked. "There was no unfinished business in my life. I was in a very contented place. All was going well. What a wonderful way to die! So peaceful, blissed out, really. Everyone would have said that I died doing what I loved. No one would be racked with grief over my death because it would have been a happy death! I could have just swum through those undersea pearly gates right into heaven's arms. It would have been a wonderful way to go!"

## Accepting His Crown

Three months later, God decided it was time to answer that question.

During the evening worship set held during a Global Awakening Healing School in the Seattle area, I felt the presence of the Holy Spirit descend on me. The sheer weight of His presence caused my shoulders to slump forward. I felt myself involuntarily edging off the seat toward the floor . . . bowing low. I knew that I was encountering a rare, holy moment; having an encounter with God Himself. I felt myself disintegrating in His presence, every molecule blowing apart. The church, the musicians a few yards away, the crowd standing, sitting and dancing in the pews behind me and around me, all disappeared. All went silent.

Just then, the rumbling voice of the Lord spoke clearly to my mind. *This is why I saved you from the bottom of the sea.*

I became aware of something hovering near to the right hemisphere of my brain—like a big bubble undulating just off to the side. The Lord spoke again. *I want to restore the anointing.* And I realized that He was asking permission to release more of His Holy Spirit, His presence into my life.

When I said *yes*, the weight lifted off and His presence broke into my entire being. Suddenly, I saw a movie-screen, close-up image of Jesus' face on the cross: the crown of thorns on His head, blood running down His face and patchy beard. The crown of thorns spoke of mockery as His tormentors abused a seemingly powerless Christ.

The gruesome image faded, and I became aware of a man sitting next to me. It was the Lord.

He took the crown of thorns off His head and held it out to me. The long spikes were familiar to me. I had seen these thorns while living in Israel many years ago, felt them draw blood along my legs, gashing through my jeans as I rode horseback near the Sea of Galilee. I drew back, hesitant for a scant second, and then reached out to take it in my hands, knowing that I would have to accept it and place it on my head. Was this the anointing? A crown of mockery? Had I not mocked myself and endured the harsh words of others long enough to burn out and sail away from ministry, church, anything religious for several years? But how can you refuse the Lord? Especially when He is sitting right beside you?

Just as my fingers barely touched the crown of thorns, it transformed into a thin band of gold. The Lord watched my expression change from dread to delight as I took hold of the crown of gold. He smiled and said, *You wear the gold. I'll wear the thorns.* Then He faded away.

I was overcome by emotion; tears released all the residual emotions associated with the thorns in my past. Soon, they gave way to joy and the courage to pick up not my crown of thorns, but my crown of gold—the crown of beauty, life, glory and honor; the crown of my calling, my future, my destiny reinstated with His spiritual authority and strength to persevere.

I had given up on God's plans for my life, tossed aside my crown of life, the royal crown that belongs to a child of God, and opted for a long vacation. But God had not given up on me. He knew the words that others had spoken against me through the years, mocking me for following Christ, criticizing me for the ways I ministered, speaking against me unjustly, words that settled onto my mind like a constricting crown of thorns.

He knew the words that I spoke against myself, the silent, negative tapes that cycled through my mind like a crown of thorns pricking me, drawing blood. He knew that all these words combined goaded me like thorns until I had

had enough and decided to toss that crown of thorns aside. He let me take my time, rest from burnout, recover from the wounds of ministry, work and life, for a while. And just as I regained my joy and was having fun hanging out in octopuses' gardens in the shade of Hawaiian seas, God decided our time would begin again.

He is the God of second chances, a second wind that suddenly fills our sails and moves us quickly across the oceans and deserts of our despair. When we cast down our crowns, or lose them by the wayside, He picks them up, holds onto them and waits. He waits until we are ready to take hold of the crowns that we think are made of thorns. He knows all along that He will wear the thorns, bearing the brunt of our pain, while we wear the gold.

Ours are the golden crowns of courage that give us dignity and strength to continue on; they are crowns of life, desires fulfilled, mission and purpose reinstated, crowns that lie across the scars the thorns left behind, adorning them with glory and grace.

> He is the God of second chances, a second wind that suddenly fills our sails and moves us quickly across the oceans and deserts of our despair.

All you need is just one glimpse of Jesus standing before you with a smile on His face, holding out your crown. Will you receive it? Will you lay down the crown of thorns the enemy impaled upon your skull—thorns that slice as deep as the scars of war, the wounds of failure, loss, guilt and shame? Will you release the images the enemy would replay again and again on the movie screen of your consciousness, as if he were rearranging the crown of thorns on your head, drawing fresh blood with every changing scene?

God has a plan established from the beginning of time—a plan to prosper you—not to harm you (see Jeremiah 29:11). And along the way, He will give His angels charge over you. Aligning yourself with these scriptural promises will unleash such a sense of peace that you can sleep peacefully in the rocking boat in a raging storm, entrusting yourself to the care of a loving Father in heaven and entrusting your loved ones to Him as well.

---

## Promise

*God will give His angels charge over you.*

---

### Angelic Interventions

God had a specific future in mind for you when you were born. His heart is for you, not against you. God does not will death; He triumphs over it. He is not willing that anyone should perish; He desires for all to embrace Him and His abundant life. God does not will disasters; but He knows how to turn them into good and create a beautiful meaning no matter what the outcome. Will He not take every opportunity to protect you and enable you to walk into your destiny?

Los Angeles minister Shawn Bolz talked to me about an experience he had involving angels. It enabled him to see how intricately God weaves the circumstances of life into events that ultimately glorify Him and transform lives:

> The Lord told me to move to Kansas City at the age of eighteen to pursue ministry there. Before I moved out of California, I took a job as a nanny for the summer to raise money to go to KC. I was caring for this woman's two boys, who were nine and seven. The nine year old had been diagnosed with ADD and was bipolar. In fact, his older brother was in a mental institution for a severe bipolar condition. As if that weren't enough trauma for the family, their oldest

brother had just died. And their father had left the family because of the stress of their situation.

I had been praying for the two boys and told them about God, that heaven is real and that angels are tangible— people even see them here on earth. As a result of our conversations, they had just asked the Lord to come into their lives. And not a moment too soon. For that week we were all going to have such an amazing experience that none of us will ever be able to forget how God intervened in our lives.

Now, prior to what I am about to tell, I'll say that I'd had visions before and had even seen an occasional angel. But never have I had such a dramatic, face-to-face encounter with an angel in the presence of others who also saw and heard the angel sent to minister to us.

The nine year old I cared for would always sit in the backseat because of the trauma of previous car accidents. In fact, during one accident, he was actually thrown out of the window of the car. And so whenever we drove some-place, I would sing in tongues because it seemed both boys liked the ethereal sound of that, and it would bring them peace.

So I was singing in tongues while I drove, and all of a sudden I saw this man coming toward me at a blind intersec-tion—really fast. I knew that he didn't see me. That man hit us, and the car spun three times and settled in the middle of the road, facing oncoming traffic. As it spun, I instinctively looked into the rearview mirror to see how the kids were. To my utter horror, I watched the nine year old fly out the window, and just as suddenly, the spin of the car captured him and drew him back into the car. I kept yelling "Jesus! No!" Then he flew out a second time and came back in.

After the old man hit us, he kept driving because he didn't know what was happening. It didn't register with him, so he drove off. He seemed to be as shocked as we were.

When the car stopped spinning, we sat there in a daze in the middle of the intersection. I noticed a man in a white leisure suit walking toward us. He looked to be in his mid-thirties, with long brown hair and olive skin (like the guy in

*The Passion of the Christ* movie). Everything he wore was white from his shirt to his shoes; and he walked over to me, pulled open the door and said, "Get the boys out right now. It's not safe to stay here."

I looked in the backseat and saw blood everywhere, all over the car and all over the boys. Replaying in my mind the older one bouncing in and out of the window, I thought, *Oh my gosh, what if he has a massive concussion? We're in big trouble.*

Then I said to the man, "No, I want to wait for the emergency crew to come and move them."

And he firmly replied, "No. Move them. They'll have no permanent injuries. They'll be okay."

Then he said, "Have peace." And I felt this incredible peace wash over me. Who ever says, "Have peace"?

I picked up the older boy from the backseat and carried him over to the side of the road. The younger one followed me and anxiously asked, "He's going to die like my older brother, isn't he?"

I replied, "No, Jesus saved us."

"How do you know Jesus saved us?"

"I just know you have a purpose in your life, and so does your brother. Jesus loves you and took care of us just now."

The seven year old told me that he had seen the man in the white suit.

"You saw the man in the white suit?"

"Yeah, he told us to get out of the street 'cause it was dangerous. And when he said, 'Have peace,' I felt calmer."

As the younger brother spoke, I noticed he became more anxious, so I told him to go back to that place in his heart where he felt the peace and stay there.

Just then, another car came through the intersection and hit my car. And another car came through, failing to see the accident, and hit the car as well. Had we stayed in the car, we surely would have died.

By now, all we could do was wait for the emergency crews. The boys' shirts were soaked in blood. My pants were soaked in blood. I had no idea about the extent of our injuries. Neither did the emergency personnel. On the way to the hospital, I felt incredible pain, but by the time we arrived, I felt fine. God healed us en route to the hospital. Once there, it was clear that whatever injuries we had sustained were almost completely healed.

Despite seeing blood everywhere in the car and all over our clothes, when the doctors checked us, they could find only a minor cut on the nine year old's head. The doctors looked at our clothes and asked, "Where did all this blood come from?"

We honestly replied that we didn't know.

The boys came out of the initial examination and turned to me for comfort, awaiting their mother's arrival. When I saw the fear on their faces, I realized that I needed to break the assignment of death off this family. So I said, "Why do you think Jesus did this for us? Why do you think He saved us?"

The boys shook their heads, not comprehending what I was asking.

"You asked Jesus into your heart, and He loves you so much that He will take care of you forever. He has a plan and a purpose for both of your lives. You will face hard things in the future, but you will go through them more easily if you remember how Jesus saved you today."

While the nine year old was getting a couple little stitches in his head and a tetanus shot, his mother arrived at the hospital, crying. But now fully at peace, her son merely said to her, "Can we go get some ice cream?"

Later, the tow truck driver showed us pictures of the car and said that when he saw the car, he was sure there was a fatality involved due to the blood and the condition of the car. One picture revealed that the initial impact destroyed the driver's side of our car so badly that there wasn't room for us to even get our legs out. How we got out was a miracle. And the fact that none of us were injured shocked him greatly.

When the boys' dad heard about the accident, God moved his heart toward home. Not long after the accident, he and his wife reconciled. In the process, both asked Jesus into their lives. And all of their boys are now living at home and being boys—but also being something more than mere boys. For they know that Jesus loves them, has a purpose for them and showed up when they all needed Him most.[1]

## Encountering Angels on Assignment

If we could only see the angels surrounding us, as Shawn Bolz and the two boys did, we would live in constant awe of heaven's ability to intervene in our lives, our families, our communities and our nations. On rare occasions, I do see angels. Every encounter has been extraordinary. Each time I have seen or heard an angel speak, it has been for a specific purpose—to release a message from God that would result in me partnering with God for an outcome that would have eternal consequences. Here are some things I have learned about angels and our encounters with them.

### Protection Comes through Angels

*Angels on assignment are often released to us not only to protect us, but to help us protect others.* One of the first times I heard an angel speak to me was during a time of prayer and soaking wordlessly in worship. The angel imparted a vision and a danger alert about a friend's young daughter. As is often the case with me, God sent an angel or heavenly creature to release an actual "movie" about an event that would come if we did not intervene through prayer. On this occasion, the angel narrated the event unfolding before my eyes on the movie screen. I saw my friend holding onto her daughter's hand while stopping to chat with another person in the parking lot of the church. Suddenly, a car sped out just as the girl wrestled free from her mother's hand and walked into the path of the car. When I told the mother about it, her maternal instincts went into high alert that week, and she was able to head off the exact scene I "saw." God gave His angels charge of the daughter—as well as alerting the mother about taking extra charge over the daughter.

Sometimes angels become visible—but other times, they stand silently beside you and you feel their presence. Many a woman has experienced that hair-raising event of sensing that her child was in immediate danger, going to check on that child and averting disaster. Was it a "mother's intuition"? Or was it the prompting of an angel? I believe angels interact with us in such ways all the time. And, if we are tuning in to the miraculous atmosphere of heaven surrounding earth, we will see them. Scripture is full of such stories.

### Preparation Comes through Angels

*Angels on assignment are often released to us to prepare us for our assignments.* While attending a conference in Kansas City many years ago, I stood worshiping in the presence of God when suddenly two small, box-shaped, many-eyed and many-winged heavenly creatures flew in front of me and unrolled a giant television screen before my eyes. I was so captivated by the creatures that I did not want to look at the screen, but the images that played out before me were so horrific that I watched in shock and the creatures disappeared. The first image was of teenagers running chaotically down the street from the perspective of a helicopter's camera pointed down on the crowd. It then morphed into big billowing clouds of white dust rolling down a city street lined with skyscrapers.

I was overcome by emotion. On the way back to my hotel room, I turned to my friend and said, "I am going home tomorrow to a major school shooting. I just hope it isn't happening in my district." I flew home on a Sunday. On Monday morning, as I sat in the principal's office of the school I was working in, the secretary popped her head in and announced that a student had gone crazy and was hunkered down in a bathroom of a nearby high school. He was shooting students and teachers. As a counselor, I was asked to go to that high school and assist with the aftermath. The images that played out on the evening news were the exact images the angelic creatures had revealed to me.

Months later, I watched in shock as the images of the billowing white clouds of another "angel newscast" came to real life on the evening news. It was 9/11, and the world witnessed the aftermath of the Twin Towers collapsing. As a counselor, I was called to attend to the schools on a nearby military base. Panicked children and teachers knew that war was imminent and were on high alert. Little did I realize that this was the beginning of my work as a consultant to the military, where I would deal with family trauma and counsel soldiers experiencing posttraumatic stress. The angelic visitation ultimately resulted in me moving not just into intercessory prayer, but into intercessory actions.

Angels prompt us into our destiny and nudge us to fulfill assignments and the purposes of heaven—whether we see and hear them or not.

### Direction Comes through Angels

*Angels are released to give us a boot in the right direction.* I have since experienced two remarkable angel visitations—both of which released direction, telling me where to go, but leaving out the details. One angel woke me up at about 6 A.M., speaking out a cryptic message: "You are going on a long voyage across the ocean." Fully awake, I sat up in bed and immediately realized that I had better get my passport renewed. I called a friend and told her the message the angel had spoken, and she agreed to go to the passport office with me. Walking up to the window, I handed over my old passport. The clerk asked me when I was going on my next trip. I hesitated for a minute, then said, "In a couple months. May, I believe."

71

When I had finished at the passport office, my next stop was the postal service where all my mail was sent. Inside my box was a letter from a friend in Rome, Italy, who pastored a rather large church. It was a request for me to come and speak at a women's retreat in May.

Why would God send an angel to prompt me to go? Because I did not want to go anywhere at that time in my life. I had some wonderful family events unfolding, and I did not want to interrupt my happiness to go out and minister. As it turned out, certain aspects of my testimony directly related to many of the women who attended that retreat. In hindsight, I would later see that it seemed a match made in heaven, where God could use the power of my testimony to break through in healing the lives of many. Needless to say, that retreat and subsequent meetings that I spoke at throughout the city of Rome were over the top with God's presence as many women were touched by God's love and glory.

Sometimes we need an angel to break through our resistance. It is easy to say no to a letter inviting you to go someplace; it is quite another thing to say no to an angel.

One of my most powerful encounters with an angel dramatically shifted the direction of my life and catapulted me into my destiny. At the time, county budget cuts had eliminated my job in the San Diego school district, and I had not made any plans to secure another job. I just had not thought such a thing would happen to me! Jobless, I knew I was soon to be homeless if I did not secure something quickly. So I made the decision to let go of my apartment and move onto my sailboat. It was not a huge boat, but it was equipped to live on comfortably. After a couple weeks of prayer and being rocked to sleep by the gentle wavelets of the harbor, I actually grew to love being in my aqua cave. Meanwhile, a friend had been prompting me to come up to Seattle to attend a Randy Clark conference that her ministry was involved with hosting. Why not? I had the time and no excuse not to go. So I went.

One afternoon at the conference, as the session drew to a close, the Brazilian worship leader who had been speaking gave an altar call for something to do with increasing the revelatory anointing on worship and the arts. As a flautist and as a writer, I went forward. The man came toward me, laid his hand on my head, mumbled a few words and moved on. Out of his shadow stepped his angel. Not a tall angel, but exactly the man's height and similar-looking to him. He was dressed in white. His countenance and the way he carried himself revealed a ferocious authority, and he had a sword strapped to his side. Utterly shocked by how fully materialized this angel had appeared to me (and how short he was), I went down on one knee, my arms open wide as if bowing before a king. It was a completely spontaneous response. I felt too stunned to speak and too overwhelmed to tremble in his presence. It was definitely a shut-up-and-listen moment.

Out of him I heard these words: "I am selling your boat when you get home. You are to be like Elisha breaking up his plow and called to follow Me. Go and pray and fast for 21 days in Redding."

Later that day, I received a call from a woman asking if my boat was for sale. She bought it. And within two weeks I had discovered that there was a church in Redding called Bethel that seemed like a good place to visit while I was in the area. I spent much of my time in their prayer house while I was in town. Eventually, I wrote an article about the church for *Charisma* magazine, which led to writing books, which led to the realization that I was now walking in the plans and purposes that God had originally intended for my life.

Do not be afraid of being homeless or jobless for a season. Even if you do not see an angel directing you, you may

He has a plan to catapult you out of your security and complacency and into your destiny!

rest assured that God has given His angels charge over you and He will never leave you or forsake you. He has a plan to give you a future and a hope. And even more—He has a plan to catapult you out of your security and complacency and into your destiny! Wait for it. Even if it seems like your journey is bizarre and friends and family shake their heads and wonder about your current state of affairs, set your heart and mind on cultivating ruthless trust and simple childlike faith in your loving Father's ability to provide for you and lead you on.

### Requesting Angelic Intervention

*We can request the release of angels and partner with heaven.* "Are not all angels ministering spirits sent to serve those who will inherit salvation?" (Hebrews 1:14). Since we are surrounded by such a great host of heaven . . . why not access God's promise for provision and intervention by requesting that the Father release His angels?

I often pray that the Lord will send His angels to go ahead of me and arrange divine appointments that will enable me to meet those whom I need to meet, to make the connections I need to make and to prearrange His favor and blessing on ministry and business situations. On occasion, I have seen or sensed the presence of angels in the room while ministering, and I have watched with amazement as the atmosphere shifted and people began to open up to the presence of God as never before. When heaven's emissaries enter the room, everything on earth changes.

I have asked the Lord to send angels to protect my daughter, and I have listened for her wild tales of divine intervention, which reinforced my belief that her loving Father heard and acted on her behalf. One evening, I sensed a heavy burden and immediately began thinking of my daughter, so I launched into a brief session of intercessory prayer until the burden lifted. During that prayer time, I asked the Lord to send His angels to watch over her, to protect her and guard her in all her ways. Later that week, she called me. Apparently, she had been walking home at night to her apartment in Los Angeles when she noticed a man following her, picking up his pace as if to attack her. She ran for her apartment, and the man ran for her. Fumbling for her apartment key, she knew that she had no chance to get the door open and shut before he reached her. Suddenly, the man stopped. A peculiar look flashed across his face, and he abruptly turned and ran away. I believe the man saw an angel watching over my daughter at the door, keeping her from harm.

## God Commands the Angels

It is one thing to pray that the Lord send angels to someone, but quite another thing to command angels. I believe that only the Lord can command His angels and heavenly creatures to do His bidding. However, I also believe that God releases some ministers and friends of His to wield His authority with special dispensation from the throne room. Here is a story the late Jill Austin, a very creative woman with an internationally known prophetic ministry, told me one day:

> While I was living in Kansas City years ago, a number of fellow itinerants were a part of Mike Bickle's church, Metro Christian Fellowship. We would try to meet periodically, when some or all of us were in town, to have times of fellowship, relationship, sharing our hearts and praying for each other. I was about to go on a six-week tour to New Zealand, along with Linda Valen, my ministry director.
>
> As I sat in the "hot seat" to get prayer from everyone, an associate pastor from the church began to share what he was seeing. He said, "Jill, there is a huge angel standing before you, and he is so tall that when I look up as far as I can, I only see up to his belt buckle!" He also made a gesture of sweeping his arm in a circle to cover the entire room as he

75

also said, "And there is a host of angels standing around the room, and they are waiting for your command."

I was intrigued and said, "I command you to go to New Zealand, ahead of me, to prepare the way for the Lord to come—and to clear away the demonic!" Several of us could see all of them leave the room for their next assignment!

When I got to New Zealand, we did a tour of six differ-ent cities, so I had been on the go for many weeks when we ended up at a church in Hastings. The meetings had been "over the top," and we were going from 7 to 10 P.M., dismissing those who needed to go home. Sometimes we continued until midnight or 1 A.M. The Lord seemed to come the most when the hungry and desperate ones stayed after the break!

A "suddenly" of God came into the meeting when the pastor's college-age daughter and the worship leader began to see in the Spirit realm. I had both of them come forward to interview them so the people could learn from this encounter. There is a "look" people have when they are seeing into dimensions of the Spirit realm—it's a look you can't fake or mimic. I was astounded that they were both experiencing the same open-eyed vision simultaneously! They were seeing and talking about the very same thing!

One of them said, "Jill, there's a huge angel standing in front of you, and he's so tall that when I look up as far as I can, I only see up to his belt buckle!" The other one made a gesture of sweeping her arm in a circle to cover the entire room as she also said, "Yes, and there's a whole host of an-gels standing around the room, waiting for your command." I was stunned that their language was almost word-for word what was told to me before I left Kansas City!

Again I said, "I command the angels to go to the cen-ter of the city of Hastings to clear out the demonic and make a way for the Lord to visit your city!" By the way, the city was named after the famous Battle of Hastings in England. As soon as I gave the command, I saw both the pastor's daughter and the worship leader turn their heads and look toward the back door. The execution of this was as if someone from the back of the church had called out their names, and they had both responded. Both of them saw all of the angels filing out and heading into the main center of town!

They were so caught up with what they were seeing that I don't think they remembered that a church full of people were watching and listening to every single thing they were saying and doing! Both of them said that a fierce battle was raging in the town square! The demons were absolutely huge . . . until the angels of the Lord appeared. Then they shrunk to their normal size and shot off into the (second) heaven, out of sheer terror, crying out for reinforcements— but none came. Many were severely wounded, they said, and wouldn't be back on active duty for some time.

They could see the Lord leaning over the balcony of heaven, so to speak, watching the battle intently, but He was not the least bit concerned about the outcome. As they were talking about the battle, suddenly both of their heads switched to the back door of the room again, and they saw the angels filing back into the church. The shocking thing was that all of the angels were ecstatic and were giving a "thumbs-up" as they came in, meaning that they had won the battle! The people erupted into deafening shouting, clapping and praise to God for the victory! Everyone there got revelation about prayer, the power of God and spiritual warfare![2]

What Jill experienced came after years of learning to walk intimately with Jesus, listening to the words that He spoke and learning to flow with Him as she ministered. Jill often saw angels and interacted with them in private and in public, so it was easy for her to enter into the experience of commanding angels. She is in heaven now, probably bossing the angels around and laughing uproariously about our inability to see with the eyes of our spirits and enter into deeper encounters with heaven—while still here on earth.

# 4

# HOPE BEYOND REASON FOR HEALING

The LORD will sustain him on his sickbed
and restore him from his bed of illness.

Psalm 41:3

Nothing seems more faith robbing and frightening than facing a doctor who diagnoses a chronic condition or pronounces a death sentence of fatal illness. Faith falters in the face of such a reality. Living with chronic pain—both mental and physical—is like taking a walk through a long, dark valley of constant trouble with nothing to lean on but a walking stick of promise that the valley will somehow lead to a door of hope. What lies on the other side of that door is a matter of constant speculation. Will the door lead to life and health on this side of heaven? Or will that door usher one past the gates of heaven and into the next phase of eternity?

People's well-meaning words hold out hope one day, despair the next. Job's comforters abound, and even best friends and relatives can say the stupidest things. But on the flip side—wonderful people can also emerge, sent like angels opening new doors of faith with words of hope. The community of fellow believers can become the most faith-inspiring fellowship. And when they come together in unity of faith, miracles happen.

When I see extraordinary miracles in the lives of the people I meet, I hear a common theme of events that contributed to their healing. First, they received bad news. Then they received personal, specific words from the Lord that contradicted the death sentence and infused them with hope. And throughout the long ordeal that tested their faith, others helped them hold onto a hope beyond reason.

The following stories are about two very different individuals who entered into a hope beyond reason, felt the support of a loving community and received a miraculous healing. One is an American pastor who was healed of leukemia. The other is an African woman living in Rome, Italy, who was healed of acute depression and psychotic episodes that she was prone to under the weight of grief. I include their stories because cancer and depression claim more lives than we care to admit. The testimonies of their healings speak to all those who have physical or mental illness that seems incurable. Nothing is incurable for Jesus. He who created us can uncreate disease and re-create health, giving us all that we need for life. Our Creator is the God of the miraculous.

Dave Hess is one of the most unassuming, soft-spoken, humble men I have ever met. Pastor of a large church in Pennsylvania, he and his family walked down a long road of debilitating illness and recovery several years ago. I sobbed my way through his book *Hope Beyond Reason*, which tells the story of his ordeal. I cried not out of sadness. Yes, the book detailed a lot of grief and pain I cannot imagine enduring, but it was far from sad. Rather, I cried because of the beauty this book revealed about faith, hope and love. Dave's faith, as he held onto the promises of God, revealed an amazing desire to live. His family and the community of his church constantly held out hope and interceded night and day for several months. Their intercessions created an atmosphere of faith that not only broke through for Dave's healing, but released a breakthrough ministry of healing throughout the church.

What brought tears to my eyes most often was the beautiful love story he wove through his book. The love between husband and wife, father and children, pastor and church, God and man splashed out from the pages and washed over me as I read. The brief synopsis of his story that I include here gives but a glimpse into how one man held onto a handful of promises and received the miraculous provision of healing.

Immediately after Dave Hess was given the news that he had advanced leukemia and needed to enter the hospital immediately, Dave heard the Lord give him a promise that implied he would not die, but would live. As he drove home to tell his family about the diagnosis the doctor had given him, he sensed the Lord speaking words of hope out of Hosea chapter 2. Here is Dave's story:

> I will allure her,
>    Bring her into the wilderness
> And speak kindly to her.
> Then I will give her her vineyards from there,
> And the valley of Achor as a door of hope.
> And she will sing there as in the days of her youth.
>
> Hosea 2:14–15, NASB

And in this valley of tears, that same Lord was opening a door of hope for me.

As I turned the corner of our street and drove toward the house, I noticed a number of cars in our driveway. Opening the door from the garage, I was welcomed by a kitchen filled with family and friends. Waves of love broke over me as I walked through the door. My parents-in-law

81

were there, along with my sister-in-law Robin. Our friend Karna and our youth pastor Tom had also rallied to the call. Upon hearing a vague report that something might be wrong, they had dropped everything to stand with us in prayer. A cavalcade of phone calls was already alerting others to pray. Within a few short hours, a small army was sounding the battle cry.

Questioning looks encircled the room. I wanted to give all of them answers. But glimpsing at the faces of Sheri and the children, I drew them aside to tell them first.

Crouching to look at them eye-to-eye, I heard myself say, "Daddy has cancer. But Jesus has Daddy."

Together we melted into one big hug, mixed with tears. We felt hands on our heads and shoulders as those we love lifted us up to the One who loves. We embraced one another, and we sensed His embrace.

A few days later, reflecting on this moment, I would write these words in my journal:

What a whirlwind this has been. Yet, what a wonderful "eye" in this storm. Promises abound in this time. Scriptures and personal words keep coming to me with the constant and sweet reminding of the Holy Spirit. There is a door of Hope in this valley of troubling! I am watching as the Lord wars against my demonic enemies (Nahum 1:2–6). At the same time, He is fortifying me with His peace, His faith, and His presence (Nahum 1:7–10). Keep rejoicing!

Habakkuk 3:19 in the Amplified Bible says:

> The Lord God is my strength, my personal bravery, and my invincible army. . .and will make me to walk [not to stand still in terror, but to walk] and make [spiritual] progress upon my high places [of trouble, suffering, or responsibility].

That night I slept like a child, safe in the arms of my Father. He is my strength. He is my personal bravery. He is my invincible army. I will not stand still in terror. Instead, I will make spiritual progress upon my high places of trouble. These words ran through my mind and out of my mouth.[1]

For the next six months, Dave lived mostly in the hospital as he battled the cancer. Twice, the doctors said he had only hours to live. Twice, Dave stepped away from death and back into life. During his weakest moments of faith, God released others with the right word to restore his hope beyond reason. Dave tells of one such meeting:

> One day a thirteen-year-old girl named Mary stepped into our lives. She had urged her mother to bring her to the hospital to see us, saying she had something she needed to tell us. Mary had been diagnosed with ovarian cancer earlier that year. A large tumor had been removed, yet doctors were uncertain about her chances for a full recovery. One day while reading her Bible, Mary came across this verse in Psalms:
>
> > I will not die but live, and will proclaim what the LORD has done (Psalm 118:17).
>
> It spoke hope to her in her valley of trouble. Here she stood beside my bed, cancer-free. The tumor was gone and Mary's life had been restored. She lived, and she was telling me what the Lord had done. Mary held out a handwritten note card with Psalm 118:17 printed on it. "I hung this by my bed when I was in the hospital," she said with a sparkle in her eyes. "It gave me hope. I want you to have hope, too. You're not going to die. You're going to live, too!"
>
> Then she prayed for us. Her words were pure expressions of trust, voiced to a God she had found to be trustworthy.
>
> With a confident smile, Mary looked at me and said once more, "You will not die. You will live. And you will tell everyone what the Lord has done."
>
> After Mary and her mother left the room, Sheri opened the mail. Included in all the expressions of support were *five* cards with Psalm 118:17 written in them. The Lord's faithful promises were calling us to a deeper place of trust! "I will not die but live, and will proclaim what the Lord has done."
>
> Together we laughed. It was not the laughter of a humorous diversion. Rather it was a confident laughter, given to

us as a gift from the Lord, born out of the relief that comes from knowing we can trust Him. He was showering us with reminders of His strong presence to sustain us. The Bible frequently says the Lord brings confirmation through two or three witnesses. We had received a word confirmed by six witnesses! I guess we needed all of them.[2]

While Dave battled in the hospital, his church battled on the home front. It has been said that nothing happens unless we pray; and that God moves mountains in response to prayers of faith. But I also believe that there is a hidden truth in the psalmist's words in Psalm 133:1–3, that where brethren dwell together in unity—there the oil runs freely down the faces of the prayer warriors, cascading joyfully out the door like the swollen streams of winter's melting snowpack, spilling over onto the streets and running into the byways and hospitals and even to nations far beyond the walls of any church building. Dave relates how his congregation stepped into a unity of spirit that released both the prophetic and healing anointing oil in their midst:

On her way home that evening, Sheri noticed that the lights were on at the church and the parking lot was filled with cars. She knew of no scheduled meeting, so she pulled in, curious to see what was going on. As she entered the sanctuary, she was amazed to see hundreds of people engaged in prayer.

At the front of the church was our dear friend Dawn Sweigart leading the charge. Dawn had surrendered her life to Jesus just a few years prior. She had come to Him with a wide-open heart that seemed to blossom overnight. She was a leader, an influencer, a motivator and a budding prophet. She heard the voice of the Lord and sensed His heartbeat in an extremely unique way. She expressed it in an equally distinctive way. We deeply loved her.

Just moments after learning the news of my illness, she rallied hundreds of people from our church and our region to pray. As a young follower of Jesus, Dawn had taken hold of His promises with tenacity. If He said He would do miracles, then He would do miracles! If He said we would do greater works than He did (John 14:12), then we will do greater works than He did! Her heart throbbed with the conviction that He will make His promises a reality in our day!

Dawn had organized round-the-clock prayer for us. People volunteered to pray for an hour each week, collectively covering all 168 hours of the week. Local pastors and their congregations joined us, and various prayer gatherings spontaneously sprang up in response to the needs of the moment and the Holy Spirit's leading. This is what Jesus said His Church would look like. More than buildings, organizations, politics or programs, He builds His Church with people. He draws those who are being rescued and restored, as well as those now devoting their lives to rescuing and restoring others.

There is nothing more beautiful on the planet than when followers of Jesus act like Jesus. On the other hand, there is nothing more grievous than when believers in Jesus don't even resemble Him. Some like to throw stones at the Church in moments like these, seeing her as detestable. Out of touch. Past her prime. But as author Fawn Parish quips, "The Church is like Noah's ark. It stinks but it's the only thing afloat." She goes on to say, "When we criticize the Church, we are criticizing something Jesus adores and spilled His blood for. It is His own precious possession."

Night after night these prayer warriors met. Often sharing in communion, they would declare the power of Jesus' victory over sin, sickness, death and all of the forces of hell. They spent hours together worshiping, encouraging one another and interceding.

But they were not just praying for me. They were asking the Lord to touch every life in our region and beyond!

Faith and fervency erupted in people's hearts throughout the congregation. Many who did not see themselves as prayer warriors boldly enlisted in this holy war. It was an all-out fight for the hearts and lives of those in our territory. Mindful of the eternal consequences, we continue to pray for every orphaned heart to know and receive the love of their Father through His amazing Son, Jesus!

What could have intimidated us ignited us.

Fresh doors of hope were being opened in this valley of trouble.[3]

Just when it seemed that the leukemia was in remission, the medical treatments caused Dave's body to react in such a way that Dave almost died—for a second time. Once again, Dave and Sheri stood and declared the promises of God, and once again, Dave stepped away from the door of death and back to the door of hope. But they still had a ways to go through the valley of trouble.

One day, Dave's appendix burst, and due to his weakened condition, doctors determined that they could not operate. They told Sheri that Dave would surely die. However, Dave had been given other promises, divine encounters with prayer, and knew that he would not die. At one point, healing evangelist Randy Clark came to his hospital and prayed an unusual prayer—not just for healing of the leukemia, but for the healing of his abdominal area. At the time, it seemed unusual. But when Dave's appendix burst, Randy's prayer became another promise to hold onto.

The doctors told Sheri that no one lived longer than a couple of horrendously painful days with a burst appendix. They could not operate due to Dave's weakened condition and decided to send him home with hospice care to die in the company of his family. But his family and friends continued to hold onto the promises of healing, and Dave continued to survive:

Finally, after six weeks, my blood levels were restored. With white cells, red cells and platelets in healthy balance, I met with the surgeon to prepare for surgery.

"I've looked over your charts," he said. "You've had a ruptured appendix inside you for over six weeks. I'm going to do an exploratory procedure on you because I'm not sure what we will find. The poison that is secreted from a burst appendix is highly toxic. We need to see what damage has been done to your internal organs."

Grateful to be alive, I underwent surgery the next morning. As I nodded off, counting backwards at the direction of the anesthetist, I remembered Jesus' promise to me. *You are a shield around me*, I said to Him as I drifted off into an anesthetic fog.

Later in the recovery room, the surgeon greeted Sheri and me. His first words to us were exclamations of amazement: "I've never seen anything like this!" Holding up four snapshots, he said, "Look at these pictures!"

They were pictures of my insides. In 5x7 glossy prints. Suitable for framing.

"Here," he said, pointing at one of the photos, "is your appendix, or what is left of it. Amazingly, it is encased inside a tent-like structure that completely encompasses your appendix! Did you ever have an operation in this part of your body?" he asked.

"Not that I remember," I responded. "Why do you ask?"

"Because this tent is composed of adhesions. It's the strongest type of scar tissue your body can manufacture. This kind of scar tissue only appears after someone has had surgery! It appears to have been in place before your appendix ruptured. All of the poison was contained inside it," he said, while making a circular gesture on the photo. "Not a drop of poison escaped this tent. Your entire internal system is as healthy as that of a twenty year old!" *What a compliment!* I thought.

Bewildered, relieved, grateful and amazed, I asked him, "What did this tent of adhesions look like?"

"That's the funniest thing," he said curiously. "It looked like a group of shields that had been sewn together!"

Just as He promised, so He had done. The Lord had miraculously created a miracle pouch. A tent of shields. Grabbing my Bible, I opened once again to the passage containing His timely word to us. I marvel at it to this day.

"Many are saying of me, 'God will not deliver him.' But You are a shield around me, O LORD" (Psalm 3:2–3).[4]

Just as God shielded Dave from death, God covers us all with His shield of salvation. Many say of those with fatal illness that God will not deliver them. Even those who struggle with chronic mental illness are deemed incurable by man or by God. Yet, holding onto the promises of God—despite evidence to the contrary—increases faith. When others draw near in love (rather than in unbelief), miracles happen. Community becomes the container of faith that holds us and shields us from the enemy's schemes. Community releases the love that empowers us to continue to hold onto hope beyond reason. Dave's family joined forces with a church community that did not waver in unbelief. And Dave was completely healed. More than ten years later, Dave remains healthy, without a trace of cancer.[5]

> When others draw near in love (rather than in unbelief), miracles happen.

While God can move and does move in response to our faith alone, the healing power seems most quickly released when a community of believers stands with the one in need.

## Community—the Container of Hope

I first noticed the amplified healing response of community while speaking at a women's retreat in Rome, Italy, some years ago. When I came in contact with another woman who was in desperate need of healing, I noticed that the miracle she received came as a result of a community drawing her into their circle of love and interceding for her day and night. This kind of love seems rare in our Western culture. Perhaps that is why God modeled it for me in the African community long before I was able to see it modeled through the Pennsylvania church in Dave Hess's story.

Elsie shuffled into the retreat, accompanied by two other African women, her eyes obviously deadened by a powerful antipsychotic. She was suicidal. Her whole world shattered when her boyfriend abandoned her and state child protection authorities took her infant daughter away until she could regain her sanity. Her African "sisters" brought her to this retreat held at an oceanside community near Rome, Italy, in hopes that God would touch her and make her whole.

Only they knew what had really happened to Elsie in her past. I could only guess what leads an African woman to leave her country, family and friends for a foreign land to earn enough money to send home and sustain, perhaps, the whole village. Poverty, sexual abuse, war and the threat of AIDS probably all contributed to her arrival in Italy, where she worked as a domestic employee in a land prejudiced against her. The stress of moving to another country is enough to unsettle anyone. Add a string of traumas occurring both before and after the move, and that pressure would challenge the coping ability of even the toughest individual. It was no surprise that Elsie's ability to cope had shattered into a million pieces.

After her breakdown, doctors on a hospital mental ward told her she was suffering from major depression with psychotic features. They stabilized her with heavy doses of medication and, several weeks later, said she could go home. Once Elsie was released from the hospital, her African friends, her sisters, took her in, watched over her, prayed for her and drew her nearer to the fires of God's love.

After several months of watching and praying over her night and day, they brought her with them to this retreat on the outskirts of Rome, by the sea, where the pastors of a large Assemblies of God church in Rome had invited me to speak. The pastors' only caveat was that I route my flight through Toronto, catch some fire at the Toronto Airport Christian

Fellowship revival and transport it across the Atlantic to them. So I traveled to Toronto and spent a few days soaking in the loving, healing presence of the Father, then reluctantly wrenched myself away to board a flight to Italy. It was here in Italy that I met Elsie and stood in awe of God, watching His presence move powerfully, healing her and many other women from depression and anxiety during the retreat and in the weeks following. It was here that I came to understand the demonic component of depression and despair and watched God shatter the "spirit of despair" in the lives of many, freeing them to dance in the fullness of joy.

Elsie was one of the first to be healed. She stood for prayer, and as I made my way down the line, she stared straight ahead as if completely unaware of what was happening. Either that or she was scared to death. I did not even know if she spoke English, but I noticed that no one translated for her into either an African or Italian language. I paused before her, raised my hand to her forehead, and before I could utter a word, she crumbled to the floor. During both the evening and morning sessions, she stood for prayer and immediately fell into a deeper encounter with the presence of God. Each time I walked on, wondering what she felt, wondering if she just fell down out of preconditioned expectation. I felt nothing. Jet lag diminished the sense of God's presence, and I just went through the motions of speaking and praying, confident that the women were receiving something of God's power and presence and prophetic words. What I felt was of no consequence. What they felt was!

The afternoon session was devoted initially to testimonies of what God was doing in individual lives so far. Two women shared freely. Then Elsie abruptly shuffled up to me. Many in the audience stiffened, afraid that she would disrupt the meeting with insane chatter. As I held the microphone for her, she testified in fairly clear English the story of her fall into sin, the trauma of losing her baby to the state, her salvation and her sense of God's presence healing her that weekend. Her African sisters sat listening, wiping tears from their eyes. For indeed, a change had come over Elsie—her eyes were clearer, and her speech, though tainted by medication, showed clarity of thought and a logical flow of content as she told her saga.

Her descent into depression originated in loneliness that led her into a relationship with a man who used her sexually—with no thought of love or commitment. As a result, she became pregnant. And when she gave birth, the authorities took away her child. It sounded similar to what David and Bathsheba experienced in 2 Samuel 11–12. The problems of illicit sex, unresolved relationship issues and unrepentant affairs always open the soul to the spirit of despair. However, God was out to destroy the works of the enemy and redeem Elsie's life from the pit, despite her having to walk through the consequences of her choices.

I stood beside Elsie and noticed many Europeans squirm in their seats while she spoke. When she finished, I simply prayed, "Father, we hear her story as a confession of how she has sinned and how You are redeeming her. Now we as representatives of the Church forgive her, and You forgive her. Release her into the complete healing You have for her. Destroy the work of the evil one that seeks to rob her of the fullness of life and joy and peace."

At that, her eyes rolled back in her head until all I could see was solid white. Rustling in the seats drew my attention and I nodded at a couple of her sisters to come up. They took her to a corner of the room and quietly delivered her of the unclean spirit that had attached itself to her during this traumatic phase of grief and loss.

On the following Wednesday night, I spoke at a large meeting in Rome and saw Elsie waiting at the door. She looked radiant.

"Elsie! What has happened? You look so full of joy!"

"Oh, Julia," she replied, "I got very sick when I left the retreat and had to go to hospital. The doctor told me that they had to get me off all medication quickly. I am healed."

Indeed, she was.

A year later, the Italian authorities refused to release her child to her custody. She fell into a depression for a short while. However, she had spent the year growing in her relationship with God and living in community with people who loved and cared for her, draping the garments of salvation around her shoulders on a daily basis. Her depression lifted quickly as she realized that "hope deferred makes the heart sick" (Proverbs 13:12), and she sought Jesus for healing. She walked through this period without medication, nor did she require hospitalization. She is fine today, coping without falling into depression . . . despite her challenging circumstances.

Dave Hess, Elsie and many others have received healing in the company of others. It is the nature of God to enable the body to "build itself up in love." When people come together, God is present in their midst. The enemy knows this, and so he moves in like a lion targeting its prey to cut it off from the rest of the herd so he can close in and kill.

Each one in these stories listened for the promise of the Lord specific to their need and declared it over themselves— or others declared it over them in intercession. Faith stirred in someone's life, and God rushed in to meet it, for God is attracted more to faith than to unbelief.

## God Will Heal *All* Your Diseases

Jesus does not want the evil one to succeed in destroying you. He wants to destroy the enemy's power over you that manifests in your life as depression and anxiety. His love for you leads you to understand that you can run to Jesus rather than hide in isolation. His love for you is even now breaking off the spirit of despair that so often accompanies long-term illness.

> Bless the LORD, O my soul,
>   And forget none of His benefits;
>   Who pardons all your iniquities;
>     Who heals all your diseases;
>   Who redeems your life from the pit;
>     Who crowns you with lovingkindness and
>     compassion;
>   Who satisfies your years with good things,
>     So that your youth is renewed like the eagle.
>
> Psalm 103:2–5, NASB

According to this passage in Psalm 103, God will heal all your diseases, redeem your life from the pit of depression and anxiety, release an overwhelming sense of His love and kindness toward you and increase your understanding of His compassion. It is part of the package called salvation.

God's Word, the Bible, is full of promises that speak of entering into the fullness of salvation. Every time I read it, God seems to make the words come alive. God speaks personally to me—through His Word and through the Word quickened to my spirit. When you are walking through the valley of trouble, reading the Word will reveal the door of hope. It will also break through any self-defeating thoughts that seek to hinder your healing and rob your joy.

*Lest you think that miracles of healing are only for special people, let me assure you that you, too, are special.*

Lest you think that miracles of healing are only for special people, let me assure you that you, too, are special. Made in the image of God, you are a child of God. His delight is in you. He does not will that anyone should suffer or be ill. If you doubt that, listen to what Dave Hess has to say about the lessons he learned in the midst of his illness.

Somewhere along the line, we have been lied to. We were told that God sends us sickness to teach us a lesson. At the same time, we were told He doesn't do miracles anymore, that He somehow "got it out of His system" when Jesus walked the earth. In fact, this lie went so far as to say if someone claims to have experienced a miracle, Satan probably had something to do with it.

I pondered this for a moment.

God gives us diseases? And Satan works miracles?

What a clever con!

This miracle we were experiencing was not a rare occurrence. In fact, what we call miracles, He calls normal. When Jesus said signs and wonders would follow those who believe Him, He did not use the word *occasionally*. And I was not getting special treatment simply because I was a pastor. He promises to give good gifts to all His children. He doesn't show partiality. He is not a shifty carnival worker who occasionally lets someone win in order to keep the rest of the customers at the counter. Though we have tried to change Him, He has not changed. He is still the God of miracles. He is still the One with Whom nothing is impossible. Nothing is too hard for Him! We can trust Him. We can hope in Him. Not because we are gullible, but because He is believable![6]

Dave and Elsie received specific promises from the Lord for healing. The promises they held onto are for you, too. But I want to leave you with something more. It is a word that God has given me for you. What if the Lord walked over to you, took your hand in His and stared steadily, lovingly into your eyes and said:

This is the year of My favor. It is the year that I will take vengeance on My enemy, who has sought to destroy your beauty and dash all your hopes and dreams. Let Me heal your broken heart. Let Me free you from your prison of darkness. I promise you this—that from this moment on I will comfort you and dry your tears. I will provide people who will listen to you and let you grieve until your tears wash away the hard lines on your face and joy steals the enemy's plans. I hold out a crown to you, My beautiful one. I anoint you with the oil of joy instead of mourning. And here! A garment of praise that I will drape across your shoulders in exchange for the spirit of despair—for you are the one I admire. My unconditional approval is upon you. I have called you by name. You are Mine. And I am yours. Watch as I do this: I will give you a double portion of prosperity and joy. The time of your suffering is over.

He is saying exactly that to you in Isaiah 61:1–3. Meditate on that Scripture, and your freedom will come quickly.

# 5

# RECLAIMING FAITH AFTER HEARTACHE

While walking along a river swollen with the melting snow-pack of early spring, near a mountain peak in the Sierra Nevadas, I asked the Lord to teach me something about faith. The river cascaded down the mountain, splitting here and there to flow around boulders and rock islands in its rush toward the sea. To my amazement, I noticed a stout little tree growing out of a rock. A seed had fallen on rocky soil, and the birds of the air had missed it! Year after year, the seedling shot its roots deeper into the rock, chiseling the rock into soil and drinking deeply from the river that swirled past on both sides. Over time, the roots thickened. The snows of winter weakened the rock, and tree root and ice split the rock wider, although it was not evident until spring. Now, the rock looked as if it might split entirely away. This little seed of faith could and would cast the rock into the sea.

It is easy to tell someone to "have faith." Quite another thing, though, to walk it out when the heavy coat of grief and loss, and promises left unfulfilled, weighs heavily against your chest and settles in for a long winter of sorrow. Even the spring thaw does little to diminish grief. It just changes the landscape. Patches of snow melt away to reveal the trail a little more each sunny day, enabling you to hike on. Eventually, the season changes and summer demands that you shed your heavy coat and lighten up. You walk more freely now. Time heals, but scars remain as silent witnesses of grief and pain that happened once upon a time.

Faith demands that you take your eyes off the scars and trust again. Trust the one whom you believe failed you; the one whose promises you think failed to come to pass. Faith demands that you release your grudge against God and let your roots sink deeper into the rock, until that rock of unbelief slides into the sea. Then you can go from moving rocks to moving mountains. Faith, once you get hold of it, seems unstoppable and feels powerful. It comes as a gift. And it moves mountains of grief and welcomes the waters of life.

Jesus never expected us to "just have faith." He always seemed amazed when someone full of faith stood before His face and reached out to grab hold of His miracle-working power. He always commented on the faith He saw. Think about His comments to the centurion, the woman with the issue of blood, the woman who needed her daughter healed, the man whose faith released healing to himself. "Your faith has healed you," Jesus often said. Or He answered, "Woman, you have great faith! Your request is granted."

The presence of Jesus inspired faith. The living water splashed out from Him and onto others, sweeping some off their feet and into the river of life.

Jesus knew His disciples lacked faith. In Mark 4:40, He said to His disciples, "Why are you so afraid? Do you still have no faith?" The very question raised their faith when

Jesus spoke it. They heard something in His voice that said, "Watch this!"

Rather than intending the question as a rebuke, I believe Jesus was simply stating what He saw in them—fear overriding faith. It was a normal human response to the situation. Any situation that enables you to see that Jesus is standing in the boat with you automatically shifts you into an extraordinary response of faith. You have faith in His faithfulness to see you through to the other side. But what do you do when you cannot see Jesus in the boat with you? Or when you feel as if He has abandoned you?

Faith is something we are responsible to stir up. It is also a gift that is ours for the asking. "For it is by grace you have been saved, through faith—and this not from yourselves, it is the gift of God," says Ephesians 2:8. And in Luke 11:9, Jesus tells us, "So I say to you: Ask and it will be given to you; seek and you will find; knock and the door will be opened to you."

Holding onto a promise from God that has been quickened in our spirits enables us to stir our faith, to ask boldly until our words become declarations of what has already come to pass in heaven and is only a moment away from being released on earth. We quell the enemy's despair-producing thoughts with, "Has not God said?" And as we speak the Word, unbelief vanishes and faith rises up once again.

Yet there are times when the journey seems too long and disappointing. Perhaps the very thing God promised did not come to pass in the time frame or manner we expected. It is then that we need a gift of faith to see us through.

Facing the loss of a loved one, especially a child, is one of the most heart-wrenching things a parent can go through. I know. I have lost both a man I loved dearly and a daughter. There were long months when I thought I could not survive the grief; weeks when I suffered through the anniversary dates of their losses; days when I wonder still if God has any intention of replacing what the enemy has stolen from me—this side of heaven. As time heals and the scars fade, I have learned how to respond better to grief and loss, and how to reclaim my faith and exact revenge on the enemy of our souls by claiming a double portion—if not for me, then through me to help heal others.

God warned us that in this life we would face many hardships and sorrows. He also promises to be with us in sorrow, gives us a comforter in the guise of the Holy Spirit and enables us to grasp hold of many lessons to be learned about ourselves and others. They are usually lessons we would rather not endure. And they leave us gasping out feeble prayers, like the psalmist who wrote, "Be merciful to me, O LORD, for I am in distress; my eyes grow weak with sorrow, my soul and my body with grief" (Psalm 31:9).

At such times, we need to ask for the gift of faith that will enable us to see beyond our disappointment in God, let go of the offense of unanswered prayer and regain hope that God will make good on His promises still. Life is hard. Jesus does warn us that in this world we will suffer and see tribulation and experience sorrow. He also reminds us that He has overcome the world and as we hold onto Him, we, too, will overcome.

How do we overcome?

First, we focus on the character of God—He is good, His love never fails, nothing can separate us from His love, He is full of compassion, He will never leave us or abandon us and He is our refuge. Second, we recognize that we cannot see the good or the glory that comes out of heartache while we are in the middle of it. Hindsight is our greatest ally. Third, we choose to practice the presence of joy! We can prepare for the heartaches and troubles to come by anticipating our response and preparing a response of faith—a response that offers a sacrifice of praise and determines not to let the enemy of our souls steal our joy. We refuse to take offense at God and cut ourselves off from His love and compassion. We decide ahead of time to nestle into Him.

100

What follows are two very different stories of couples who had a promise of God about their children yet to be born, fought for their children and overcame the plan of the enemy. Sherrie and Steve Brown were told their unborn child would likely be severely retarded, but they held onto a promise that quickened their faith. Their child was born healthy—despite the doctor's original diagnosis and hints that they should abort the child.

Another couple who attended my former church believed that they had received several promises from God about children they would have. In the meanwhile, she suffered through two miscarriages. Rather than take offense at God for not fulfilling His promise to them of long-awaited children, they reacted in faith—reclaiming their trust and hope in the Lord in the aftermath of heartache.

These two stories reveal both couples' remarkable reactions to the dire circumstances they faced and Jesus' equally remarkable response to their faith.

Here is Sherrie's story:

My family and I entered the ultrasound room and waited for the doctor. After having several ultrasounds of my growing womb, the thought of yet another sparked some apprehension. Even though my own doctor assured me the reason for this ultrasound was to find the exact size of my baby girl, Jesse, I was still a little unsettled. The ultrasound doctor came in and introduced himself. He immediately began his procedure and was specifically searching for something in her skull. Within minutes he told us our daughter would have a good chance of severe mental problems, and my husband and I would need genetic counseling.

Fear began to wrap itself around me like cords, pulling me into its world; however, faith rose up to rescue me. I immediately felt a surge of power rise from within and was released from these paralyzing feelings.

I glanced at my husband, Steve, to see how he responded after hearing this startling news. With one glance from Steve's eyes, I knew he was strengthened by the Lord and was extending that comfort to me. I then looked at the doctor and declared, "Dr. Smith, I am 44 years old. I don't have a left ovary or tube, because I was diagnosed with endometriosis when I was 22. My husband, Steve, had a vasectomy reversal four years ago, and I appreciate the information you shared. However, we are Christians. I know my husband would agree with me when I say to you that our daughter is a miracle and that she will be fine. At least now we know how to further pray."

The doctor appeared momentarily disoriented. The news I had shared startled him, and he quickly responded, "You're 44 years old!"

He was kind and sincere in his further remarks, letting us know that he, too, would pray for us, but that we still needed to make an appointment for genetic counseling. The doctor completed the ultrasound and handed us a video, and we made our way out to the front desk.

The waiting room was crowded with women and other couples. This particular ultrasound facility was for women who had problems or concerns with their pregnancies. My curious eyes made their way across the room and placed themselves on a young couple who were apparently in tremendous distress. Their faces wore their concern. I quickly thought, *Perhaps they, too, have received similar news and are struggling emotionally.*

Normally I would have approached the couple to pray right then; however, the Holy Spirit placed His hand on my heart and let me know that it was not the time. My son Jordan, Steve and I made our way to the desk to schedule our appointment for genetic counseling. After doing so, we left to find our car and make the long journey home.

As soon as we got in the car, I called four different couples and asked them to pray for us. I spent little time with details and made sure they knew we felt this to be an assignment from the enemy to destroy our faith, rob our peace and kill our joy. After all, that is Satan's job.

Steve maneuvered the car to the interstate, and I reflected on what had just transpired. The Holy Spirit reminded me of two powerful messages. They were tucked away in my heart for such a time as this. He spoke, "Remember, Sherrie, f-e-a-r is false evidence appearing real." He also reminded me, "Faith is believing what you cannot see will come to pass, and fear is believing what you cannot see will come to pass."

I shared with my husband what the Lord had spoken. We knew that giving way to fear would take us down a road that would only bring discouragement. We had to let faith take over in order to regain the peace we had carried before this doctor visit. Together we proclaimed that our miracle daughter was perfect and that no weapon formed against us would prosper.

That evening I spoke with a very close friend from Idaho. She said, "Sherrie, I believe the Lord wants you to pray the armor of God onto Jesse." I did so right then. We finished our conversation quickly, and I headed for bed. I was exhausted by the emotional and mind-bending day.

> "Faith is believing what you cannot see will come to pass, and fear is believing what you cannot see will come to pass."

The following days were not easy. I wrestled with the enemy's constant assaults directed at my mind. There were visions of Jesse being retarded, and my body was harassed by what felt like continual surges of adrenaline.

The Lord spoke once again. He said that I was to cancel the genetic counseling appointment. I heard His voice gently speak, "Going to genetic counseling is preparing for Jesse to be brain damaged. Believe what you have declared and prayed for. She will be fine."

Sunday arrived, and we traveled to our church with expectancy and joy. After the message, I went forward to receive prayer from our pastor's wife, Sheila, and daughter Sylvia. They immediately began praying, and as they did, I felt the peace of God wrap around me like a warm, soft blanket. I was aware of the Holy Spirit's presence, for God's power rose within and gave me strength. My once-tormented mind and body began to feel enveloped by God's love. I felt His loving consolation abide in me.

After we finished, Sheila chuckled and said, "That's funny; while I was praying I saw the armor of God on Jesse." Sylvia chimed in with a joyful voice, "I was just going to say that. I, too, saw this." I had not shared with them about my friend's suggested prayer over Jesse previous to this. I knew it was confirmation of the Lord's protection over our precious baby.

I had three more months until Jesse would arrive. I was delighted that these months were free from the agitations I had felt previously. I carried the assurance in my spirit that all was well with my soul and my baby.

February 13 arrived, and so did Jesse Shelah Brown, born at 9:15 P.M. and perfect. She is four years old now, and one of the smartest little girls I know.

## Joy in the Midst of Grief

The other couple whom I want to share about, Ron and Jenny (not their real names), were married in their late thirties and could not wait to start a family. While praying about when to start a family, each one felt God gave them specific Scriptures about the children they would have and gave them details about their children's lives, from their names to their spiritual gifts. Here is their story of faith:

> Within a year after their honeymoon, Jenny discovered that she was expecting, and she and Ron immediately spread the good news about her pregnancy. *Here comes the promised first child!* they thought. Their joy was short-lived, however. Within two months, Jenny miscarried. They were heartbroken.
>
> Not long after, Ron's mother died, leaving him a nice inheritance. With the funds, they spent the next two years

building a house. Ron also switched jobs, becoming a day trader in the stock market. Then the economy sank into a downward spiral, and Ron's stock market speculation led to greater losses than he could imagine. Along with the financial chaos, Ron and Jenny found themselves battling fear and depression. They wondered if they would be able to hold onto the house and decided that trying to get pregnant again was not an option during this hard season.

In an effort to buoy their faith, they turned to the Word and underlined Scripture after Scripture of encouragement. They prayed and fasted, seeking God for favor and strategy that would enable them to recoup their losses and get out of the financial bind. Jenny never gave up on her dream of starting a family, and as she read, she also underlined the promises she felt were from God about children—specifically applying the words to her life—believing, in faith, that she would soon have the family she desired.

It was not long before Jenny discovered that she was pregnant once again. This time, she kept the pregnancy a secret. She knew that once she let others know, their well-meaning comments and phone calls would elevate her joy. And if she miscarried, many people would have to be told—and repeating the story of loss in the middle of her grieving would be too difficult. She decided to wait until they reached the three-month mark. The wait was excruciating.

During that first trimester, a man with a recognized prophetic ministry came to speak in their church. Ron and Jenny attended the meeting and were thrilled when the prophet picked them out of the audience and asked them to come forward. Once on the platform, the man gave them several words about the ministry God was calling them to and prophesied that Jenny would have a child very soon . . . even twins . . . a double portion to cover her previous loss! Stunned, she knew the prophet had no idea about her miscarriage. So she took the word to heart and began letting people know that she was indeed pregnant. All of her friends thought surely this was the long-awaited child.

After all, she had several promises from Scripture and even the word from a prophet.

They took the words and stormed the gates of heaven with declarations of God's goodness, claiming that this child would be healthy and live, and declaring that this was the beginning of their dreams coming true.

But it was not to be. It happened again. Within a couple of weeks, she miscarried.

Jenny crawled into the cocoon of her house, disconnected the phone and disappeared from contact with her friends and family for a while, shielding herself from their comments. Day after day, she poured out her grief to the Lord and sought Him for answers to the question we all ask after losing someone to an untimely death—*Why?*

The Lord sat beside her silently while she poured out her heart. After a few days, spent emotionally, Jenny began to hear His voice speaking softly to her heart.

*I love you. I am with you. Offer up a sacrifice of praise.*

She had expected Him to answer the question *Why?* Instead, she just heard that He was there, with her in the midst of her heartache. No excuses for His lack of intervention. No answers as to why she lost the child. Certainly not a response that would lift the grief and give her hope for the future. Or was it?

As she meditated on the Lord, it dawned on her that God did not will her miscarriages. Eventually, she knew that God would open her eyes to see the good that He would bring out of the situation—but not during the season of grieving. It would come later.

She knew that blaming God would only set her up for a lifetime of anger, bitterness and depression. She also knew that somehow, offering the sacrifice of praise would begin to set her free.

Jenny began to worship and praise God for His faithfulness to her. She thanked Him for being with her; for never leaving her or forsaking her; for not being moved by human need but reserving the release of His perspective for another time and place. She declared that she would trust the Lord no matter what the future held, and that with or without children, she would rejoice in Him. She still tucked the promise of a family away in her heart but gave the outcome to God, giving Him permission to create that family in *His* time and in *His* way.

Eventually, she heard that whispering voice of God speaking His Word into her heart once again:

*The joy of the LORD is your strength.*

Jenny was being called to a higher level with her praise and worship—that of practicing joy when she felt the lingering heaviness of grief.

Sometimes people are so caught up in despair and anxiety that they forget God is near. They memorialize their pain and grief and focus more on that than on a testimony of God's healing love and presence. Believing that they will not recover, they are caught in the whirlwind of unbelief stirred up by the enemy of their souls. The only way to break through that whirlwind of pain is to stop agreeing with the disparaging thoughts of the enemy and begin offering a sacrifice of praise and thanksgiving.

As Jenny found out, a sacrifice costs you something. When everything in you sees nothing to be thankful for and your emotions run rampant, offering up those thoughts and emotions on the altar of thanksgiving is a sacrifice. Rather than focus on discouragement and lies, use every ounce of discipline in those times to offer a

> The only way to break through that whirlwind of pain is to stop agreeing with the disparaging thoughts of the enemy and begin offering a sacrifice of praise and thanksgiving.

sacrifice of praise and thanksgiving. It is not easy! If you have no words of your own to pray, try using the words of this psalm as a sacrifice and offering. It will move you in the opposite direction from your present negative thoughts.

How kind he is! How good he is! So merciful, this God of ours! The Lord protects the simple and the childlike; I was facing death and then he saved me. Now I can relax. For the Lord has done this wonderful miracle for me. He has saved me from death, my eyes from tears, my feet from stumbling. I shall live! Yes, in his presence—here on earth!

In my discouragement I thought, "They are lying when they say I will recover." But now what can I offer Jehovah for all he has done for me? I will bring him an offering of wine and praise his name for saving me. I will publicly bring him the sacrifice I vowed I would. His loved ones are very precious to him and he does not lightly let them die.

O Lord, you have freed me from my bonds and I will serve you forever. I will worship you and offer you a sacrifice of thanksgiving.

Psalm 116:5–17, TLB

Practicing the presence of joy is the ultimate way to reclaim your faith after experiencing heartache.

## Practicing the Presence of Joy

Many people go through such horrendous times that it seems impossible to praise and give thanks for the hell they endure. I do not wish to trivialize their pain. As a trauma counselor, listening to people's stories would often spin me into a daze—stories of war and torture, rape and abuse. Stories from Africans, Cambodians, Middle Easterners, even Americans. "What reason do they have to dance? To practice the presence of joy? How can they?" some would ask. But I know that others, no less the victims of evil, would answer, "How can they not?"

I have watched Israeli warriors dance the folk dances of the psalms, giving praise and thanksgiving for deliverance. One older man in particular raised his hands as he danced; his sleeves pulled back just enough to reveal the crude tattoos of

numbers on his forearm. After his release from a concentra-
tion camp during WWII, he gained enough strength to fight
for a homeland, a place where his people could live in peace.
He celebrated life as he danced. The pain of the past receded
as dancing released joy within him.

Another man I saw while I was living in Israel during the
late 1970s impressed me so much that I will never forget
him. He stood near a coffeepot and chatted with other kib-
butzniks, members of the community. I could tell from the
way the others approached that they held him in high regard.
This man radiated love and light and joy like no one I had
ever seen before. Laughing at something the men shared,
the man turned to pour himself a cup of coffee, exposing
his forearm, exposing the past that had seared his flesh but
left his spirit soaring.

On yet another kibbutz I witnessed a less resilient group of
survivors. They had survived the Holocaust, only to shatter
into a postwar psychosis from which they would never recover.
One woman, led by an attendant to the dining room table,
shuffled up to her chair, her head snapping left to right, her eyes
vacant. She sat down, staring straight ahead until the attendant
brought her a plate of food. The woman leaned forward, her
hands guarding her plate. As she rapidly shoveled the food into
her mouth, her eyes kept vigil left to right, lest someone try to
steal her food. Abruptly, she pushed her plate away and stood
up, hopping from one foot to the other until the attendant led
her away, long before the others had finished eating.

What was the difference between the joy-filled man and
this woman? Both survived unspeakable Nazi terror. Only one
chose to leave the past behind and enter into the appointed
times of feasting and celebration. Only one chose life. And to
fully embrace life, he must have dealt with his past. I imagine
that he grieved the loss of many family members, faced the
loss of his youth, watched men die and no doubt killed a few
himself as he fought to establish a homeland. Yet he pushed
through the grief, forgave his enemies and forgave himself.

Light stole the darkness from his heart. Joy conquered the pain. And he danced and laughed and celebrated life—more and more every year. Somewhere along the healing path, this man had encountered God. He radiated God. Somewhere in his journey, he had received the abundant grace of the Lord, who delights to reveal Himself, to reveal His nature. This man felt the touch of God, and it was so healing, so delightful, that he was forever captivated by God's love, choosing to live life with God.

### Choose Life—Choose to Live

Do you want to shatter the enemy's plan for your life? Stop colluding with the thoughts and fears that play like a broken record in your mind, and choose life. Are you thinking of death as the peaceful end to all your troubles? That is exactly the strategy of the one whose mission statement is to rob, to kill and to destroy! (See John 10:10.)

Choose life. Choose this day which god you want to align yourself with—the one who brings death or the God above all gods whose mission statement and name is "the way, the truth, and the life" (John 14:6, NKJV).

If you want to break free of the spirit of despair and find freedom from grief and loss, pray this simple prayer out loud—or better yet, write one of your own similar to this:

> Father of Life, I choose life. I choose You.
> Thank You for the power of Your love releasing deliverance to me.
> Thank You for Your mercy and Your kindness.
> Thank You for always thinking of me.
> Thank You for being the kindest Person who ever lived and walked on earth . . .
> who forever lives and always thinks of me.
> Thank You for times of joy and celebration coming my way.

110

Thank You for Your presence filling me with new life.
Thank You that You have a plan and a destiny for
me,
that I am a wanted child, Your beloved.
Thank You that I can run to You, and You always
embrace me.
Thank You that I am not broken beyond repair.
Thank You that You are restoring trust.
Thank You that You are enabling me to forgive those
who have wronged me.
Thank You that You are enabling me to forgive
myself.
Thank You that all things will work together for my
good.
Praise You for Your deliverance.
Praise You, for Your nature is full of goodness.
And Your intent toward me is one of providing love,
peace, joy, supplying all my needs.
Praise You for Your redemption, that You are lifting
my life from the pit.
Praise You for Your gentleness and for Your justice.
Praise You, for You are great and powerful, and yet
You know my name.
I choose life.
Now come, Lord, release to me the joy of Your
presence.

# 6

# HE CROWNS YOUR FAMILY WITH SALVATION

Deep inside the Father's heart rumbles a longing for all to recognize the sacrifice He made in offering His only Son as the salvation of the world. His heart cries that all should be saved, and it echoes in our spirits as we continuously discover the fullness of salvation released in our lives and desire that others should know Him, too. Everyone who has encountered personally the love of God longs for those in his or her family to come into that experience of salvation readily available to us all. Mothers long for prodigal children to return. Sisters and brothers desire more of a unity that comes from the Spirit rather than the tenuous bonds of the family bloodline. Blood may be thicker than water, but a family that has entered into the unity of the Spirit through Jesus becomes an even stronger conduit of love.

We ache for our earthly families to reflect heaven's original intentions. And when someone steps across the line into self-destructive, sinful lifestyles, goes prodigal or dies an untimely death, we often wonder if they are beyond the reach of heaven; if it is too late for them to enter into salvation or if they missed their only opportunity to surrender their lives to Him. We have no idea when God will intervene in their lives. Certainly not in the timeline that we have established. God's ways are not our ways. Yet He knows how to move heaven and earth to weave us all into His divine plan for salvation.

During those times of wondering, we need to hear the promise of our family members' salvation straight from the Lord.

After years of separation from a daughter whom I had lost to adoption during my senior year in high school, my heart still ached for her. No mother can forget her own child. Every one of us, unless we are deeply mentally ill or severely drug affected, wants the best for her child and needs to know how he or she is doing. Long separations create an undertow of emotions that can drag us into the sea of despair. It is during those times that we need the promise of God that He knows and sees and will act on our behalf and on behalf of the one who is missing.

On the anniversary of my daughter's birthday one year, I felt her loss worse than in other years and cried out to the Lord for her salvation and safety. In reply, the Lord gave me a Scripture that seemed to leap off the page and embed itself so deeply in my heart that I knew I could trust Jesus.

The promise He held out to me was that my daughter would return leaning on the arms of a son . . . (see Isaiah 60:4).

It made no sense to me at the time. I had no sons. She was my only child. I tucked away the word in my heart and trusted God for the reunion I longed for. Years later, my future son-in-law encouraged my daughter to develop a relationship with me. Indeed, she came back leaning on the arm of my "son."

Yet, in the years that I have known her now, my heart still longs for her to know Jesus as intimately as I do, to be healed of any pain that she endured in her early years and to enter into the fullness of salvation—life abundantly, dancing in the fullness of joy. My heart's desire for her is that she should know the Lord. I needed to hear another word directly from the mouth of God that would put my heart at rest. God, with His Father-heart full of the compassion of knowing what it feels like to be separated from His Son, heard my whispered prayers and set up a moment of divine intervention that would put my heart at rest.

One evening while I was attending a little church meeting, a prophet named Bobby Conner walked by me and said, "God is going home with you. Your whole family will be saved."

I thought that was odd. After all, I am single and live alone. Then Bobby's face took on a quizzical look, and he spoke again. "I mean your lineage. Your lineage will be saved."

My lineage—the flesh of my flesh—will be saved! My heart rejoiced at the thought that my daughter will come to know Jesus. And then it dawned on me that the word *lineage* implies more than one generation. A few years after Bobby gave me that word, my daughter has still not yet come to know Jesus. But in the meantime, she has had her own daughter. And deep inside of me, my heart is at rest because I know that one day, whether I live to witness it or not, they will both be saved and living in Christ.

## Promise or Relinquishment?

Those are special moments when Scripture leaps out of the page and instills hope in our hearts or when another person gives us a prophetic word that crushes unbelief and jolts us into faith. We take hold of the promise and pray the Scripture back to the Lord—"Lord, Your Word says this! I believe it! Bring it to pass." And time marches on—usually bearing little witness to God moving in response to our prayers of declaring His Word. Meanwhile, something is happening behind the scenes. God's ways and timing are not what we would like, and we grow discouraged. What do we do then? Do we continue to claim His promises, or do we give up and relinquish the dream?

If you believe that the word you are holding onto really arose from God's will rather than your own desire and self-will, no matter how well intentioned, keep declaring His goodness and faithfulness to bring it to pass. But if you reach a point where your prayers sound tired and demanding and you feel as if God is even more distant than when you first began to pray, another tactic may be in order.

*Relinquishment is the act that says, "I trust You, Jesus."*

Try praying the prayer of relinquishment. Walk up to face your fear full on and consign even that possible outcome to the care of your loving God. Surrender to the possibility of what you fear the most. Surrender as an act of ruthless trust, knowing that God's love will ultimately be enough to cover you. Relinquishment is the act that says, "I trust You, Jesus. And I trust that whatever You allow to happen to me or to the one I am praying for, Your love will keep us all close to Your heartbeat for now and through eternity."

At that instant, fear leaves. Peace creeps closer. Love tiptoes in. The prayer of relinquishment surrenders all control to the ultimate love and unseen intentions of God.

I have had to pray the prayer of relinquishment often for my family. I continually gave my daughter to the Lord from the day I realized as a teenager that I could not care for her. My own home was breaking up in many ways, and I had no place to bring her home to, nor did I have the support I felt I needed to raise her. So I relinquished her to the Lord and to adoption. And in all the silent years afterward, I prayed often for her, giving her to the care of the Lord. It was only after we met that I leafed through my prayer journal and realized that the most intense times of prayer for her synchronized with the days of her greatest need and deepest hurts. God's hand was surely upon us both. Even in the years after our reunion, I continued to give her to the Lord. She is His. She always has been.

We claim promises for our children and loved ones, but ultimately, they are in the care of God. And God's home extends far beyond our galaxy.

What follows are the stories of three others who heard the Lord speak to them about lost family members. They have learned how Jesus would have them cope with the loss of a family member. One dealt with a daughter who became a "Dead Head," another lost a mother as a result of suicide and the third lost a brother in the aftermath of AIDS. They, too, have witnessed what good the Lord could bring out of such untimely deaths. Lee Peavey, Barbara Yoder and Paul Keith Davis have much to share about their encounters with Jesus in the aftermath of the destruction in their families of origin. Let the promises the Lord spoke to them become promises the Lord holds out to you, too.

## A Mother's Fight of Faith

Lee Peavey seemed to have the perfect Southern family, and when her daughter, Allison, was born, she felt as though all her dreams were coming true. It was not long before her dreams were tested and she began the fight of faith for her daughter's life. Lee told me her story:

> "At the age of ten weeks, Allison was going to die of bronchial pneumonia," Lee explained. "So the hospital staff packed her in ice, and the doctor told me that if she wanted to live, she'd live." The family mobilized their spiritual resources, and Lee, weary from watching her infant struggling

to hold onto life, released her to the Lord—for the first of many times to come.

"After she was in the hospital for a week, I came to the point in prayer of saying, 'Lord, if You want her, You can have her,' " Lee related.

The Lord wanted her, indeed. But He wanted her alive. And in the process of surrendering Allison to the loving care of Jesus, Lee realized that her daughter would always be God's child.

All through school, Allison seemed to be the perfect child. She was a leader in her church youth group, an excellent student, a beautiful child who was destined to become a stunning young woman. Yet Lee sensed that Allison's relationship with God seemed nonexistent at worst, or distant at best. She saw her daughter going through the social motions of attending church and being "good" but really saw no fruit in her life, no evidence that God was something more than a social construct. And Lee knew that Allison's tenuous spiritual bond would not sustain her in the days to come.

According to Allison, "I was never saved. I kept saying the sinner's prayer but had no relationship with the Lord, and the subject of Jesus made me uncomfortable. I just loved the social aspects of church, yet at the same time, I saw things in my church and school that did not exemplify Christ. I was full of judgment and offense."

By her senior year in high school, Allison craved popularity and started drinking with the "in crowd." She took a job working at Hallmark and began partying with her co-workers, as if to make up for lost time.

One night shortly after graduating from high school, Allison came home with a friend, a stack of horror movies and an astrology book. Lee woke up in the middle of the night. Sensing a deep foreboding, she launched into and almost involuntarily travailed in prayer. She somehow knew that there was a demon in the house and got out of bed, walked toward the downstairs den and called out to the girls, asking what movie they were watching.

"I could see the astrology book, and I said, 'You need to stop watching that witchcraft movie,' " Lee said. A power struggle ensued. At first glance, the battle seemed to be a classic case of mother against daughter. However, we fight not against flesh and blood, but against principalities and powers. That night marked the new beginning of a battle that would last more than ten years in a classic case of mother against demon.

Lee told Allison that she needed to remove the movies and books from the house immediately. Allison refused. By the end of the night, Allison had moved out of her parents' home and into a house with other co-workers. Over the next six months, she would return to the house only to steal money when her parents were not there.

"I just wanted to have a good time," Allison explained. "I was smoking pot and dropping acid. I definitely had an addiction to many drugs."

Lee realized that her daughter needed her to be strong, and she determined that no matter how Allison treated them, she would always open the door to Allison and welcome her home. So Allison bounced in and out of the house for a few years. She lived there for brief periods of time, until her addiction drove her away from home.

"We could not have a conversation without an argument," Lee said. "When she was home, I hated to be there. I dreaded going home to confrontations with Alli. My husband and I had an awesome marriage. But during that time, we disagreed about how to handle her. He was mercy, and I was tough love. We never had to kick her out because she would just leave. But I did keep the checkbooks locked away because I did not trust her. When her wanderlust kicked in, she always left. But through it all, I held onto one promise, a Scripture that came to me time after time."

The promise Lee held onto was this: "Train up a child in the way he [or she] should go, and when he is old he will not depart from it" (Proverbs 22:6, NKJV). She believed Allison would turn around and surrender her life to the Lord any day. However, the worst was yet to come.

Allison started dating a guy who led her into her first arrest for smoking pot in his car. Scared and angry, she left town before the court hearing and started hitchhiking alone from her home in Alabama to Colorado. A van full of hippies picked her up and took her to her first Grateful Dead show in Kansas City. They gave her drugs and a ticket to the show.

Suddenly, Allison felt like she was finally where she belonged and knew that she was right smack in the middle of attaining her destiny as a "Dead Head." She felt as though she was called to hang out as a dead groupie, following the band around the United States, going where the tour led her. She ended up in a homeless shelter and eventually called Lee to get her back home to take care of the hearing.

"Most of the time during Alli's ten years on the road, I didn't know where she was. During those first three years of her wanderings, I prayed daily for her salvation, and I began to question if I should have done something differently," Lee said. "All my friends' children were doing well, going to college, getting married. Mine was not. Yet, I had a strong faith. And I knew that the prayer I prayed when Alli was dying as an infant still stood. I continually gave her to the Lord and proclaimed that there was purpose in her life and that the Lord's plans and purpose for her would prevail. And at one point I heard the Lord speak to me and say, 'She will be Mine.'"

All the worst scenarios a mother can imagine flooded Lee's mind as she fought in prayer for her daughter's life. "I didn't know where she was, but desperation led me to another crossroads in prayer, and I found myself saying, 'It doesn't matter what it takes to bring her back to You—I give You permission, Lord.' I had to give all my fears over to Him," Lee said. "It took time, but eventually I entered into a place of total peace, and I knew that she would eventually be in heaven with Him."

God protected Allison in that season. She would emerge very different in personality, but she was spared all the horrible things her mother imagined and fought against in prayer. She never overdosed. Nor did she find herself pregnant or riddled with sexually transmitted diseases. She didn't end up accidentally killing someone while driving under the influence. Nor did she end up with a jail record. God's angels surely moved in response to Lee's intercession and protected the young woman.

Allison continued her Grateful Dead tour for several years, making and selling dresses and bean burritos and selling drugs in the parking lots of the shows to support herself and stay on tour with a van full of friends. She styled her hair in the fashion of the culture—long dreadlocks that she wears to this day. She was completely immersed in the life of a family-oriented hippie culture.

Eventually, the drugs and the constant wandering wore Allison down. She reached the turning point while staying in a trailer near Bend, Oregon, in the midst of a weed-growing operation.

"I woke up in the early morning on the floor, a dirty shag, peed-on carpet. I hadn't had a shower in I don't know how long. I was hungry, strung out and out of drugs," Allison related. "When I looked around the room, I saw no one who really cared about me. I felt a moment of clarity and thought, *I am 27 years old. I am smart, pretty and I am in a trailer, strung out. I have parents who love me. I am going home.*

"Because my parents never said no to my coming home, when the time came, I knew that I could go home and change. I knew that they would always welcome me home," Allison said. And so she called her parents one day and told them she was coming home.

Lee and her husband told her, "Come on, then."

Going home was easy. Change takes time. Despite the fact that Allison had a full-blown heroin addiction by then, God released His healing power to her and she never experienced withdrawal. She met the man who would become her husband and eventually realized that she needed more than a man; she needed Jesus.

One night while Allison was reading in the book of Romans, she started crying uncontrollably. Thinking that she was having some sort of breakdown, she decided to call her mother.

"It is so like God, that after all those prayers, He would allow me to be the one to lead her to Him," Lee said. "It

121

wasn't like Allison didn't know who Jesus is. She was ready. I came to her house and said, 'It's not going to get better until you let the Lord be Lord of your life.' We talked for an hour, and she said she was ready. I led her in the sinner's prayer. She was so excited and so overcome by God's love that I knew her salvation was real."

To this day, Allison and her family are walking with the Lord. Allison teaches in a Christian school in Kansas City, and alongside her husband and two children, she ministers to other prodigals.[1]

## Hold On—He's Coming!

Barbara Yoder is the co-founder and an apostolic leader of Shekinah Christian Church in Ann Arbor, Michigan, a thriving, multicultural and multigenerational church she inherited from her late husband. Barbara still marvels at the way God met her early in her life and turned her from being an intellectual prodigal into one who is deeply beloved by her Father. Here is her story of the encounter with Jesus that led her "home" in the aftermath of her mother's suicide and enabled her to bring the rest of her family with her:

During my childhood, I lived in the middle of the evangelical revival in America. Billy Sunday's widow was our neighbor. People traveled from all over the nation, as well as the world, to hear great leaders such as Billy Graham, Bob Pierce (founder of World Vision), V. Raymond Edman and others speak at Billy Sunday Tabernacle. Later, we moved and became part of one of the more influential churches in the nation. It had great strength and supported more than thirty missionaries. We were excited to be involved. My parents often hosted guest ministers in our home, great men and women of God at that time. Some were world leaders. I grew up listening to the greatest preachers, some very compelling and fiery. I tried really hard during my entire childhood to find this God they kept describing. Since I was a sensitive child, I kept listening intently to all that was said. But I could never find God in a way that satisfied my heart. Apparently, neither could my mother, for she suffered from a very serious depression that ultimately caused me to lose faith in God and caused my family to flounder.

We didn't know about the power of God available to heal and deliver. I'd sit by my mother's bed, holding her hand, watching her sob all day long. In fact, one summer I stayed home to take care of her. As I watched that incredible emotional suffering, it made me wonder why God would allow this to happen to anyone. My mother had been a wonderful person. Eventually, I stopped trying to find God. I just didn't want to serve a god who would inflict such suffering on someone. My ultimate break with God was soon to follow.

Shortly after I turned eighteen, my mother committed suicide. People callously said that her death was *the will of God*. Back in those days, everything was attributed to *the will of God*. Months later, the pastor who led that great mission-sending church we had attended committed adultery. The church community became like Sodom and Gomorrah, for when the head falls, the people follow. Was that in the will of God, too? My faith felt like it had been demolished by those two pivotal events.

I totally trusted that pastor and the church that had made such an impact on our family. Now that I had lost my mother and the church, I fell apart. Finally, I decided to turn against religion; it was too frustrating and just wasn't real to me. I couldn't experience a real encounter with God; it was all about head knowledge and nothing about the heart. As a result, I didn't believe any of it was real.

I became a temporary atheist. I say temporary because Jesus always had His hand on my life and knew that the desire of my heart was to know Him and experience His presence. He didn't leave me wandering in the midst of my own despair for too long. He knew the plans He had for me. He knew that one night He would walk into my room and like Saul, I would experience my very own Damascus Road type of encounter with God. All of my head knowledge would go blind as I would feel the overwhelming love and presence of Jesus begin to heal the wounds of my heart.

In the meanwhile, I became an intellectual's intellectual . . . very heady; totally unemotional. I'd have to watch a sad movie once a year just to try to cry and release emotions.

Eventually, I became a professor and taught at the University of Wisconsin. On the outside, I appeared totally successful. My life looked great. I skied on the weekends and worked hard all week, loved my students and was on the right academic track.

I was a voracious reader and studied both contemporary and historical philosophers—Nietzsche, Kierkegaard, Kant, St. Augustine, anybody I thought had something to say to both Christians and non-Christians searching for answers and reality.

One night, I sat up reading Dietrich Bonhoeffer's book *The Cost of Discipleship*. I read somewhere in the book about having to take the leap of faith. That phrase, *the leap of faith*, caught my attention. I cried out loud, "God, I don't know how! Jesus, if You exist, I have a few things to talk over with You."

Suddenly, I saw Jesus walk into my room. When I saw Him, I started crying uncontrollably. He said nothing. He just stood there. His presence emanated the power of His healing love. At that point I felt a door deep inside open up, and all the pent-up pain and grief started to pour out. I cried and cried for a very long time. I felt from Him such love. I felt the reality of His existence. It was so powerful that I have never questioned the existence of God since that night.

The encounter itself felt as if it lasted all evening. It was as if Jesus came in and just kept continually washing over me with His incredible love.

I called my father the next day and told him about my encounter. He was thrilled because he had thought I was going to hell. I was running with a fast crowd. The first thing my father said was, "Do you remember what this woman said to you in church when you were a child?"

"I never forgot it," I replied.

And he said, "Neither have I."

One Sunday when I was eleven or twelve, this woman at church caught my eye and stared intently at me. Then she found my parents and asked them if she could speak to us. We were strong evangelicals at the time and had never heard of prophecy, praying in tongues or anything like that. This woman put her hands on my shoulders and told my parents that she had been in prayer and God told her I was going to raise up a great work for God. We had no idea that was prophesying. What she said was so extraordinary that none of us ever forgot it. Although my father and I reminisced about the moment, it would take awhile before we understood the full meaning of her words.

The first great work of God seemed to focus on my immediate family. Because of my own healing, I was the one who began to lead my family into a new faith in God, which eventually restored the family's faith after my mother's suicide.

My father, knowing what had happened to me, began to open up to the touch of the Holy Spirit. At some moment in time, he had his own encounter with God. One night the Lord appeared to him and simply told him that he wasn't responsible for my mother's death. Now, my father was a very private man, the top engineer in his field in the state. Normally he would keep his emotions to himself; however, he wanted each of his children to know what happened to him. So he called me and told me how God appeared to him and told him it wasn't his fault. He was very emotional as he spoke. That one encounter with Jesus took that burden of guilt off him so that he could live with peace. And he was a changed man from then on.

My family hadn't split apart, but they were all intellectuals. My brother had lost his faith and was going in a wrong direction. I got into prayer over my brother. While in prayer, the Lord told me what to do: call my brother, tell him to come visit me and then lead him into a new relationship with God. He was working on his Ph.D. at Duke University at the time. While with me, he experienced an overwhelming encounter with God and was baptized in the Holy Spirit. God so gripped his heart that he took a year off to live with me and learn about God. To this day, he remains a devoted believer who loves God. Later, a similar thing happened to my sister.

Despite my encounter with God, I was aware of an absence of God in some ill-defined sense. Every once in a while, the pain of my mother's death came back. Gradually, as I learned to access God's presence and power, total healing took place. I had to work with each aspect of the loss. I found that I grieved not only over her death, but also over her not discovering how much God loved her. She died in an unfulfilled state. I discovered that God takes each one of us through a unique process. Our process teaches us about God and enables us to "buy things" for others. The healing and knowledge I had gained bought healing for my family. The healing kept unfolding.

The final puzzle piece wasn't pain over the loss, but my pain for my mother's pain. One day, the Lord showed me that I had been carrying this grief around, a grief over my mother dying without discovering what I had found out about God's healing presence and power. Once I worked through that final piece of the puzzle, the process was completed.

Sometimes it takes years to work through some things, and God is so faithful to take us through the process. Because I've walked through that process of healing, I understand other people's pain in a way that few do. I am able to walk with them without heaping guilt on them. Many people are not able to access God in the midst of their situation or their grief, and they need direct divine intervention to break through to God's peace.

Hebrews 5:1–2 says that He takes His ministers or priests from among men so that they will understand the pain, the weakness, the infirmity; and it's a different word in different translations. He takes us through a specific process so that we understand others' weaknesses, their shortcomings; so that we can reach down and lift them up; so that we're approachable.

We're not God. We're human beings who have been touched with pain and weakness and doubt and unbelief so that people can grab hold of us. I often say to people, "You cannot find God right now, but just grab hold of my faith until you can access faith directly yourself." And it works. Sometimes people just grab hold of me for a season.

That moment when God walked into my little home and introduced Himself to me now forms the foundation for my whole life. When I go through tough times even now, I look back and rehearse that situation of how God intervened in my life and walked in and revealed Himself to me, faithful to see my healing through. Faith begins to arise as I realize that I may not feel God's presence the moment I need Him, but He is on the way.

Somehow God found me when I couldn't find Him. So I know He will always find me. And He will find you, too. He's coming! Just hold on.[2]

Barbara's story reveals a specific key to increasing your faith—look back and remember when and how God met you in the past. Hold onto your personal history with God and recall those times when He revealed Himself so clearly to you.

If you have not yet developed a personal history with the God of the miraculous, the God of the personal—Jesus who loves you beyond all that you can imagine—then hold onto the other stories in this book. Hold onto Barbara Yoder's story and declare that the goodness of God is reaching out to your family. Ask the Holy Spirit to hover over your loved one and love him or her into the Kingdom of God. Surrender the process to Jesus, and let Him work a miracle in your family, too.

Faith begins to arise as I realize that I may not feel God's presence the moment I need Him, but He is on the way.

127

All Things Are Possible . . .

Even if you believe that it is too late for someone in your family to come into the awareness of God's love, even if you are unsure if he or she is really saved, know this—God is able to reassure you that He has that person all wrapped up in His saving grace. Let this next man's story encourage you to know that with God all things are possible, as Scripture says:

---

### Promise

*When the disciples heard this, they were greatly astonished and asked, "Who then can be saved?"*

*Jesus looked at them and said, "With man this is impossible, but with God all things are possible."*

Matthew 19:25–26

---

Paul Keith Davis, a former businessman called by the Lord into an internationally recognized prophetic ministry, wrestled for a long while in prayer, questioning God and longing to know if his recently deceased brother actually made it to heaven. Eventually, God granted him a remarkable vision that settled his heart. He tells the story:

My younger brother died of AIDS at the age of 32. I always felt that Robert was saved, but I had this nagging doubt in my mind after he died—what if he wasn't? Despite the fact that he lived with us during his last days on earth, I just wasn't sure. The Lord knew that it weighed heavily on my mind, and one night, He graciously enabled me to have a spiritual experience through a vision that put my fears to rest.

For many years before he died, my brother worked in Birmingham, Alabama, at the children's hospital. Unbeknownst

128

to him, a witch coven had actually assigned themselves to come against the children's hospital in 1995, and the woman who led the coven also worked in the hospital. Eventually, she recruited him into her little group. Eventually, she also passed on the HIV virus to him.

All Robert knew about the Lord was what he learned in the Baptist church we were raised in as boys. When he left home and made his way in the world, he really knew nothing about the spiritual realms and how actively the enemy seeks to devour, kill and destroy—anyone he can get his hands on. Robert lived in rebellion against what little he knew of the Lord and dismissed salvation as a quaint religious idea promulgated by the church.

One day, Robert went to a séance. It was there that he got demonized. He had long ago left the church, and he never quite understood why I had changed my life so dramatically when God called me out of the secular business world into the prophetic ministry. We talked some about the Lord over a period of time, but Robert couldn't hear anything about the Lord Jesus Christ. The spirit he had given himself over to was not the Lord.

My brother was the most handsome one in the family. But contracting HIV changed all of that. I don't know if you have ever watched someone die of the virus, but it is not an easy death to view. Not many deaths are. Despite the demonic spirits that sought to isolate him, Robert took us up on our offer to love him and take him into our home during the worst season in his life.

He lived with my wife and me for several months, then with my mother before he died. Part of that time, we ministered to him as the demonic hold on his life manifested and attempted to torment him on the way to the grave. It was not uncommon to hear the bed moving across the room as the demons manifested. So we would go in, pray and set him free. Eventually, we got him completely free from the demons, as well as free from the spirit of fear. But it was a tiring process. We had high hopes that God would completely heal him. We prayed for more. Yet Robert wasted away as his immune system slowly shut down.

By the time he died, I believed that Robert had experienced a genuine salvation and that he felt the peace of the Lord carry him straight into the arms of heaven. But was that what I wanted to believe, or was it really true? In my grieving his life and his death, I often pondered the question of whether he made it to heaven. But God didn't let the question linger too long on my mind.

A few months after Robert died, I was in prayer when suddenly the Spirit of the Lord caught me up into heaven. Immediately, I saw an open field and realized that I was walking along with this staff in my hand. Most of the vision had to do with things other than my brother—things pertaining to the Church in these last days and the supernatural anointing, that mantle of Elisha that is about to be released to this generation . . . and already is.

Then I saw some people coming up to me who were absolutely illuminated with glory. I peered more closely at them, trying to discern who they were. One of them was my brother! I couldn't believe it! I said, "Robert, I can't believe you are here."

I knew I was seeing a vision. I said, "Robert, have you seen the Lord?"

He said, "Oh yeah. He is so beautiful."

His response was kind of unusual. His face was glowing, and he seemed so joyful. It wasn't the same Robert I had known on earth. I was astounded at the transformation.

I had a question on my mind for the Lord and wanted to ask Him face-to-face, but I realized that in this vision, I was not destined to see Him. So I said, "Robert, next time you see the Lord, ask Him—"

But Robert interrupted me. "Now, don't you do that. You know there is no mediator between God and man except Jesus."

Apparently, Robert's knowledge of the Word had greatly expanded during his few brief months in heaven. I remember being surprised, but also put in my place.

We embraced, and that was the end of the vision.

But it gave me absolute assurance that Robert was there.[3]

No matter what the spiritual state of our family members, we may all hold onto one promise—the promise that God is very aware of what is going on and is able to intervene when we least expect it and often without us even knowing about it. Isaiah 65:1 says, "I revealed myself to those who did not ask for me; I was found by those who did not seek me. To a nation that did not call on my name, I said, 'Here am I, here am I.' "

Keep asking God to reveal Himself to those in your family who are not even seeking Him. When God says *Yes*—you will know.

# 7

# THE BLESSING OF CHILDLIKE FAITH

I will never forget the time I met Mahesh Chavda, an internationally known healing evangelist. As part of my research for an article I was writing about his ministry, I was attending a conference held at his home church in South Carolina. Perched at the edge of the stage, mopping his brow after praying for dozens of people, he tilted his head and looked at me.

"Come here and give me a hug," he said.

I really was not interested in hugging a large, sweaty, silver-haired man in a conservative preacher's suit who had a prophetic knack for knowing exactly what was going on in someone's life. It did not even feel like a particularly huggy moment, so I thought it an odd request. But I complied.

As I leaned toward him, I suddenly tumbled into Narnia, feeling the way my three-year-old niece must feel when she innocently hugs her dad, laying her head on his shoulder, without a care in the world, absolutely secure in his presence. And all I wanted to do was lift my little hand up and touch his face. I felt myself being gently pushed away and realized that I was also feeling quite woozy. The presence of God released through Mahesh impacted me greatly. I stood before him absolutely stupefied, in an altered state of consciousness, unable to carry on a normal conversation because the power of the Lord came so gently and deeply upon me.

Days later, I realized that the hug was one of the most profound spiritual experiences I have ever had. It healed something deep in my heart that had to do with trust, innocence and wonder. The childlike ability to embrace faith, lost somewhere along the road to adulthood, had been restored. The hug also gave me a glimpse of Mahesh Chavda's heart that no lengthy interview could impart. This man had learned to love by ministering for years to severely mentally and physically handicapped children, holding them and asking God to release His love through Mahesh's touch. And he knew that only love can make a miracle of healing happen in any of our spiritually handicapped lives. He knew that just one brief encounter with God can change everything.

What if Jesus walked up to you and said, "Give Me a hug"? Would you? Can you even imagine it? Or have you completely lost your sense of trust, innocence and wonder along the rocky road to rational adulthood? Have you become spiritually handicapped in the process?

C. S. Lewis's Chronicles of Narnia have led more adults than children into a greater revelation of the personality and nature of God. His series helps readers go "further up and farther in" to the Kingdom, experiencing realms of the Spirit through the eyes of four young children who tumble through a wardrobe in the ordinary world straight into the wondrous world of Narnia. Through these books, the deep truths and miracles of the Kingdom are not revealed to the wise and learned, but to children—or, more to the point, to the child hidden within us all; beneath wrinkles and aches, financial responsibilities and relational stressors, the child who longs for release into another Kingdom (see Matthew 11:25).

Even still, those of us who read Lewis ponder ways to step out of our everyday life and into the extraordinary realm of the Kingdom of heaven. How do we get there? According to Matthew 18:2–4, the one who approaches Jesus like a child is the one who will enter into the deep things of God, eyes open to seeing the realms of heaven, spirit ready to receive the deeper truths of who Jesus is and what this life is all about:

> He called a little child and had him stand among them. And he said: "I tell you the truth, unless you change and become like little children, you will never enter the kingdom of heaven. Therefore, whoever humbles himself like this child is the greatest in the kingdom of heaven."

The childlike ones joyfully delight in visions and increase in faith as they see miracles working in everyday life.

Children receive instruction without debating the outcomes, hold your hand when they cross the street, jump up in your lap just to cuddle and speak so freely about what they see and hear that it bypasses the defenses of adults. They enter easily into the Kingdom of God because their young hearts are wide open to fresh experiences. Every day is full of new adventures. Every adventure creates a longing to see, hear and touch more and ask a thousand *Why?* questions as they try to process their awe and wonder at the mysteries of life unfolding before them.

Children not only seek to understand the natural world, they are spiritually alive. A child looks at the sky and wonders who made the stars. From the mouths of babes, unexpected wisdom leaps out to stop adults dead in their tracks with some truth a child could not possibly have known. Children are back-door prophets who slip in behind adults' defenses and surprise them with prophetic and revelatory words.

Some children chat with angels. Some bounce on beds while talking to Jesus; some receive just the right "word of knowledge" that unlocks the heart of an adult, opening it up to receive Christ. Children venture as a group into realms of heaven, and some have been so powerfully touched by God's presence that their touch passes the power of God along to others. God always initiates these experiences, and He always has a purpose in mind before releasing spiritual experiences to children.

As you read the following stories about children, let their innocence tenderize your heart and awaken a longing to experience the Kingdom of God as easily as they did—by simply receiving and enjoying encounters with Jesus, angels, dreams and visions. Let the purity of these children's experiences and experiential knowledge of the deep truths of the Gospel lead you into an increased faith to encounter God in fresh and real ways. Revelation of and from the Kingdom of God is yours today.

---

### Promise

*The promise of God to you is this—if you become like a child . . . you will venture deeper into the Kingdom than ever before . . . for blessed are the pure in heart—they will see God (see Matthew 5:8).*

---

In recent years, the Holy Spirit set the hearts of children and teens aflame in small groups across the United States and Canada. Their passion, in turn, ignited a childlike faith in adults to enter into their own God-encounters and to release the presence of God into their spheres of influence.

### Children Encountering God

In 1988–89, a sustained move of God came upon the sixth-grade class at Dominion Christian School in Kansas City,

Missouri, and spread to the rest of the students. During this move of God, these kids experienced angelic activity, meeting each other in the heavens and having visions, out-of-body experiences and fresh insights into the love of Jesus and His realms of heaven. Their encounters drew their parents, along with other adults, into the school. As the adults walked into the atmosphere of heaven descended upon earth, they, too, became like children and encountered visions they never dreamed would come to them.

The school happened to be affiliated with a large church called Kansas City Fellowship, a church that not only believed such things could happen, but welcomed spiritual experiences. During that time, I went to Kansas City as part of the ministry team accompanying John Wimber, former pastor of the Anaheim Vineyard Christian Fellowship. We held a special ministry time at the school for the children and watched as the power of God engulfed many of them, laying them out on the floor and releasing visions of Jesus and heaven.

Later in the evening, a couple of the children came to the house where I was staying, and I asked them what they had seen and felt. A three-year-old girl said, "I saw angels like in a movie. And then I fell asleep."

"What did they look like?" I asked.

"Like this," she replied. Holding her little fingers in front of her, she wiggled them and spread her arms wide, lifting them upward as if shimmering angel wings took flight before me.

I knelt down to her level as I asked, "And what did you feel?"

She cocked her head as if annoyed by questions she did not have the vocabulary to respond to, thought for a moment and then stretched out her hand until it touched my forehead. "Like this," she said as the most exquisitely sweet and delicately loving presence of God flowed down through my head and body, making me feel light as a feather that could float to the ground and not feel a thing upon impact. It was the kind of feeling I could imagine Jesus giving to young children to bring them into revelation of how loving and kind He really is to everyone. And, come to think of it, the child's touch imparted the same feeling I felt years later when I hugged Mahesh Chavda and tumbled into Narnia as my heart opened to experiencing the Kingdom of God like a child.

Along our information superhighways of Internet reporting, and through many charismatic conferences, people are talking about an increasing number of children's encounters with God. Children are lifted up to heaven to romp and talk with angels, or they see angels in their rooms at home.

One mother in Louisiana confided to a Christian co-worker (a friend of mine who later told me the story) that her eight-year-old son seemed to be having spiritual experiences. He claimed to see angels and even Jesus. She entered his room one day and saw him bouncing on his bed, talking excitedly to some unseen guest. Laughing, he told his mother, "I'm talking to Jesus." His astonished mother then heard him say that she was going to have another child soon. A few weeks later, she discovered that she was indeed pregnant. The child's foreknowledge helped the mother to cope with current life stressors. Neither of the parents are Christians, but they are accepting their son's unusual, ongoing encounters with the realm of God and his new gift of predicting the future. Before long, they may enter into their own encounter with God.

Jennifer Toledo, director of the Global Children's Movement, believes that the Kingdom of God belongs to the child-like. The humble faith of children is powerful enough to melt the hearts of adults hardened through years of pain and disappointment. The innocence of children can move mountains.

In her ministry to children in other countries, Jennifer trains children to be "naturally supernatural," teaching them to worship, intercede for others in prayer, minister to the sick, pray for their healing and speak prophetic words to those they meet. She has seen the response of non-Christian adults—normally resistant to other adults who are preaching to them—soften when approached by a child.

Jennifer has much to share about reaching out to the lost, abused, broken, starving children of other countries and turning them loose to impact the transformation of their own communities and countries. She tells the story of Richard, a nine-year-old boy from the Turkana tribe in northern Kenya, who found his way off the streets and into a missionary home. Richard was selected to lead a team of twelve children into a local hospital, where they were encouraged to minister to the more than one hundred seriously ill and dying patients crammed into a tiny room. At first the children seemed overwhelmed by the sights and smells that hit them as they walked in. Everyone turned to look at them, and the group turned suddenly timid as nervousness set in. They looked at Jennifer, unsure of how to proceed outside the comfortable surroundings of their ministry training center. Jennifer simply knelt down and told Richard and the team to ask Jesus what they should do. She tells what happened next:

After a few moments, little Richard tugged on my arm and whispered in my ear, "I think I'm supposed to sing a song." I smiled at him and placed him up in front of the other children. He looked around the room, and everyone was silent as they stared at him. He closed his eyes, turned his heart toward Jesus and began to sing the hymn *I Surrender All*. As he worshiped, he lifted his hands toward heaven and tears began to stream down his face. It was the purest, most beautiful worship I had ever heard. As he began to worship, the presence of God came and filled the room in the most amazing way. All over the room people began to weep under the conviction of the Holy Spirit. By the time he was done singing, the presence of God was so strong in the room that there was no other ministry that needed to be done. Every single person in the room cried out for salvation and wanted to know this Jesus that Richard was singing about. Because of his simple obedience and his pure worship, lives are being transformed. Richard has gone on to be a big part of community transformation. He has inspired many people to begin investing in and releasing children. Richard is still worshiping, and still knows that one day he will be a pastor.[1]

## Creative Healing Power

Just as God uses little children to lead big children to the Lord, He also demonstrates His healing power in children through creative ways that adults sit up and take notice of. The following story has sparked increased faith in adults to receive healing encounters with God as they take time to meditate on being with Jesus in heaven, receiving what they need from Him in the throne room or in the garden and bringing it back to earth—much to their surprise.

Karla Johnson, a pastor's wife, was told this story by a dear friend whose son encountered Jesus in heaven and brought His healing back to earth:

> When our family began attending Troy Vineyard Christian Fellowship in Troy, Alabama, our son Joshua seemed to absorb everything taught about the Holy Spirit. He jumped at the chance to be trained and participate in the Children's Prophetic Team at church outreaches. Several adults in the church even noticed how prophetic he was by the impact of the words he gave. Ten-year-old Josh would look up, smile and deliver a profoundly simple, encouraging word to church members or even to complete strangers.
>
> Josh was very spiritually minded, but in the natural he had struggled with serious allergies all of his life. As an infant, he cried constantly. When he was two weeks old, the doctors switched him to soy formula to try to alleviate his vomiting, hives and eczema. Doctors immediately suspected allergies, but they were at a loss to determine the cause. Next they recommended hypoallergenic formula, but even that caused a reaction in Josh.

Our local doctor finally referred Josh to Children's Hospital in Birmingham, where they diagnosed his allergies. At one point we were paying $23 per can of formula, but at least his symptoms had subsided. Dairy products, tomatoes, citrus, soy, wheat, seafood and all nuts were life-threatening to Josh, and we never went anywhere without an EpiPen just in case Josh encountered an allergen.

I became very adept at dealing with Joshua's condition. Every thought was consumed with what he could eat or what he might encounter in everyday life that is benign to most of us but was possibly catastrophic for our son. I longed to walk through the mall and relax, but I dared not venture there because of the perfumes and peanut butter cookie ingredients wafting through the air. We had tried it once just to get out as a family, but simply walking through the cosmetic department of an anchor store to return to our car resulted in Josh vomiting and needing Benadryl by the time we reached the parking lot.

Simple joys such as being held by his grandmother were rare for him since her perfume would cause a reaction. We shielded him from seafood being cooked or the smell of peanut butter because either would mean another night spent at the emergency room. It seemed that even when we tried to protect him, an allergen would attack from an unsuspected source. We once attended a family fish fry, thinking Josh would be safe because the fish were being cooked outside. We were wrong. All of his usual symptoms ensued, and we left the reunion for the emergency room.

Josh's sister, Sarah, knew that if she ate peanut butter at a friend's house, she had to brush her teeth and wash her face, hands and mouth well before getting near Josh or their brother, Matthew, who has many of the same allergies. But one day an innocent kiss after a peanut butter snack sent Josh into a reaction.

Family and friends talked about us being too good to hang out with them, but they didn't understand that Josh's need for protection outweighed our desire for relationship. It was a difficult, lonely time for us all.

In December 2006, the nurse from the elementary school called to say Josh was having a reaction to something, but they hadn't been able to determine the cause. An investigation revealed that someone was serving peanut butter down the fourth-grade hall. If it was enough for us to smell it, it was enough to send Josh to the emergency room, even after two EpiPens and 50 milligrams of Benadryl.

Then God sent us an angel. On June 1, 2007, Judy Franklin of Bethel Church came to our church to teach her Going to Heaven seminar.[2] My husband and I didn't really know what to expect, but if it was of God, we wanted to be there. Since our small church sometimes doesn't have childcare at special events, Joshua joined the adults in the sanctuary—and I am so thankful he did!

Judy shared about her first experiences of going to heaven, and that God told her to remember how she got there so she could bring others. At the end of the second session, she played a CD and led us through a series of steps to go to heaven. Different people shared their experiences as we journeyed deeper into the encounter, and Josh quickly volunteered to share about playing baseball with Jesus. He spoke through his broad grin as if it happened every day of his life.

The next morning in children's church the pastors led the elementary-aged group in another session of going to heaven. Josh lay on the floor and closed his eyes. He noticed that Jesus had set up a picnic table for them. On Josh's plate was a big slice of pizza.

"What's that for?" Joshua asked the Lord.

"It's for you."

Josh said, "But, Jesus, I'm allergic to pizza."

The Lord told him, "It's okay, Josh, you can eat pizza in heaven." Full of faith, Josh laughed, talked and ate pizza— wheat flour crust, tomato sauce, cheese and all, "like a normal kid"—in heaven with Jesus.

After church, Josh nonchalantly related his experience to the family. We thought it was wonderful, but I sensed God wanted to give him much more than just a nice memory. My husband and I had been reading *When Heaven Invades*

*Earth* by Bill Johnson, so I told my husband, "You know, we're supposed to bring heaven to earth." He agreed, and the wheels in my mind started turning.

Sunday evening I decided to make smoothies for the kids, as I often do for family time. Normally, I would make a special smoothie for Josh using Rice Dream, a non-dairy ice cream substitute, and ginger ale. Remembering what Jesus told Josh in heaven, I realized this was my opportunity to bring heaven to earth. I made all the smoothies the same without telling anyone.

Josh downed the first one and thought it was so good that he asked for another. Prior to his experience in heaven, Josh would have regurgitated any milk product immediately, followed by labored breathing, swollen lips and hives. I looked at him and discreetly checked his lips for swelling. He was fine, so I made him another smoothie.

After half an hour passed uneventfully, I informed my husband of my experiment. Then I told Josh to read the ingredient list on the sherbet that went into the smoothies.

"I ate all this?"

"Yep, you sure did."

We were all amazed. Josh called the children's pastors and several other leaders in the church to share his story immediately, and the testimonial buzz began in our small southern town. The following Sunday, the children's pastors served cheese biscuits in honor of Josh's healing, but his comment was, "Can I just have a plain one? I've been eating cheese all week!"

Jesus rescued us from the grips of a monster that had entangled our family for ten years. I no longer have to read every ingredient declaration or fear for his life when he goes to school. Josh spent the night with a friend for the first time in his life a month after his healing. We are free!

Our family has been through some trying times since Joshua's healing, but whether the needs are finances, jobs or relationships, my husband and I know that we can walk through them because if Jesus healed Josh of all those allergies, then He can walk us through anything.

Members of our church have shared Josh's testimony repeatedly, believing that the testimony of Jesus is the spirit of prophecy (see Revelation 19:10). When someone says that they doubt healing is for today, they love to say, "Well, let me tell you about a boy in our church." We believe that God is using Josh's story to tear down the spirits of religion and unbelief that rail against believers in our region of the country.

Joshua still goes to heaven often, and I'm glad. I want our son not only to walk in his healing, but to walk in the supernatural naturally. I want him to know that his healing is only the first of many miracles His Father will allow him to walk in. I pray Josh never loses that ability to enter the Kingdom of heaven.

I absolutely do not advocate that parents ignore medical advice and rush to test the healing they believe their children have received, as Josh's mother did. However, his story has encouraged many who have heard it to reach out in faith and access the healing they need, too, as Josh and his family did.

## Childlike Faith for the Miraculous

Children often lead their parents into deeper levels of faith by talking about their own experiences with God. It is as if God looks for the one with the most simple faith and delights to reach out and touch him or her, creating miracles just because He can. Read on and who knows—perhaps your child's encounter will become something that transforms your whole family and causes your faith to soar.

Brandi Wilson's son experienced an answer to prayer that transformed Brandi. Her anguish over another son with severe handicaps turned into faith for his healing. As you read his story, let Spencer's childlike faith become your own.

My husband and I have five children. Spencer is our second-born. Spencer is a cute kid with the most beautiful red, curly hair I've ever seen.

One Sunday our family got up to go to church, as usual. Nothing too exciting happened that morning. As we made our way to the car, we noticed that it was extra windy, but we didn't think too much of it. We had four kids to buckle up in car seats, so there wasn't a whole lot of brain power used up on the wind.

We went to church, and it was great. On the way home, we stopped to pick up some lunch to eat at the house. As we pulled up in our driveway, we were stunned at what we saw. There was a huge tree lying down in our yard. The strong wind had knocked over our tree. That tree had been planted in our yard longer than I had been alive, and there it was, broken off at the base and sprawled out across the grass. As we got out of the car, holding our take-out lunch, my husband and I were in awe of the Lord's protection. The old mulberry tree covered our whole front lawn. It fell inches from our house, but it did not touch it. We were so thankful that the tree didn't land on our neighbor's house or their car. It just fell perfectly in our yard, as if someone had set it down by hand.

My husband and I began to thank the Lord for His protection, but Spencer was excited about something completely different! As he barreled out of the car, he was yelling, "God did it! God did it!"

We were confused, so we asked Spencer what God had done.

He was thrilled to report, "I asked God on the way to church to blow down our tree so I could play on it because I'm too short to climb up it, and He did it! God did it!"

Immediately Spencer ran over to the tree and began to climb all over it. He was as happy as he could be. He knew that God heard his prayers. Mark 11:23 says, "I tell you the truth, if anyone says to this mountain, 'Go, throw yourself into the sea,' and does not doubt in his heart but believes that what he says will happen, it will be done for him." I guess in our case this Scripture could have the word *tree* substituted for *mountain*.

God blowing down our tree at Spencer's request just added to his mountain of reasons why he believes God answers prayers. Our youngest son, Miles, has cerebral palsy. He's almost three, but he's still at the developmental age of about a one-month-old. This little boy Spencer of mine, who knows that God will blow over trees for him, continues to pray every single day for complete healing in his little brother. Recently Spencer told me that he couldn't wait for Miles to walk. He said that he knows that Miles is going to. As I was listening to him, I wanted to be more like him, so I asked him *how* he knows that Miles is going to walk. He said, "I just know."

Matthew 18:3 says: "And he said, 'I tell you the truth, unless you change and become like little children, you will never enter the kingdom of heaven.' "

God, I know that faith pleases You! I know Your Word says that we need to become like little children to enter the Kingdom of heaven. God, make us more like children!

On our mantle sits a framed photo of Spencer climbing on the tree that the Lord blew down for him. When we see it, we are all reminded of how even the winds obey God. What a glorious day it will be when we get to place a photo next to that one of little Miles walking into the arms of his big brother, Spencer!

## Come Like a Child

Children are curious beings. If they were not, I would worry. I would be concerned if they were sitting alone in a corner, failing to enter into the company of others and experience new things day to day. If an adult loses his or her spiritual curiosity, goes off to his or her own corner, retreats from anything new and fails to experience the freshness of each day, I would say that that person has leveled off spiritually and maybe even died.

A child's heart is open to fresh revelation, new understanding and increased experiences. Children embrace all

146

that life has to offer them every day. When you lose that child's heart of humility and excitement and think that you have become an expert in the things of God and life, you level off in your development and stop growing. The more mature you are, the more childlike you should become in receiving the things of the Kingdom of God. When you shift from ongoing

The more mature you are, the more childlike you should become in receiving the things of the Kingdom of God.

dependency on Him to an attitude that you can handle it from here, that you know all there is to know and can do things for yourself now as one who is all grown up, you lose the innocence, dependency and wonder of being with Him.

Who is ready for the next revelation of God? The child. The child who stays hungry and excited about discovering new things; the child who knows that all good things come from the Father.

Receiving the Kingdom of God like a child implies trust—trust that the Father will not give you a counterfeit of the Holy Spirit, a rock rather than a slice of bread, a false vision designed to bring confusion, an experience that makes you feel tainted rather than excited to be in His presence. You have a childlike confidence that your loving Father is indeed speaking out of the vast universe to little you.

Come like a child and tumble into Narnia. As we allow the experiences of children to lead us into the deep truths of the Kingdom and a greater revelation of the personality and joy of Jesus, know this—it is the Father's good pleasure to give you the Kingdom, too. All of heaven is open to you. It is time for you to ask for more revelation and come further up and farther in to the realm where you can see angels, hear Jesus, experience more of the gifts of the Holy Spirit and walk with the spirit of wisdom and revelation every day.

# 8

## RECOVERING COMMITMENTS TO MARRIAGE AND MINISTRY

While studying marriage and family therapy at a Christian university, I decided to intentionally observe couples interacting in public. I had seen more broken families than healthy families in my lifetime. I had seen couples from Christian homes and secular homes divorcing and even pastors leaving their spouses and their ministries, so I knew how easy it was for a marriage to fall apart and for people to give up. Not many couples seem to have truly happy marriages. I started wondering what makes a happy marriage. The question most on my mind as I observed couples was this: Why do marriages survive? And I wondered how couples in ministry manage to remain committed to their covenant of marriage under the overwhelming stress of serving God in pastoral ministry.

As an avid sailor, I had many opportunities to watch couples who had just spent a weekend or a whole week together cruising the Pacific Northwest waters. As they came home and approached the dock, their interactions spoke to me about the way couples work together and handle long periods of togetherness in a confined space. After a while, I realized that couples powered into the dock with one of two attitudes—they either could not wait to get away from each other and spoke harshly to one another, or they seemed to slide into the dock in harmony with one another, roles defined and rehearsed, comfortable with one another's ways. It is clear that most marriages fall into one of two camps—mutually encouraging and honoring, or mutually destructive and dishonoring. Couples are either committed to the journey together, or they cannot wait to jump out of the boat.

Some "captains" among the sailing couples snapped at their partners, berating them for not handling the lines correctly. Some wives, anger and resentment twisting their faces into scowls of disappointment, were poised to jump off the boat and run away as soon as they landed. Others slid easily and peacefully into their moorage, working in harmony with one another, wordlessly in touch with the nuances of each other's signals.

Working together as a couple is clearly difficult. The more practice, the more peace—or so I thought. The old adage "practice makes perfect" really does not apply to marriage. Practice may create a façade of peace, but one man's peace is another man's boredom or results in a passive-aggressive interrelationship. Marriage, at least the public persona of a marriage, is so much more complex that I decided that I would stop observing couples from a distance and start doing some "man on the street" interviews.

Imagine walking up to a couple and saying, "Hey! You look a little angry at each other . . ." and engaging them in conversation. Not wise, and not likely that they would respond kindly to the intrusion into their private lives. I decided on another tactic. I would talk only to those who appeared to be in a good mood, seated and relaxed, clearly enjoying each other's company.

Church seemed like the ideal place to conduct my interviews. Many of the people I talked with about their marriages gave me variations on a single theme. One attractive, middle-aged couple I talked to really summed up what so many others echoed. I noticed them sitting in front of me in church, whispering and smiling, his arm stretched easily across the back of the pew, caressing her shoulder. During the greeting time, I casually engaged the wife in conversation. I let her know that I was a grad student studying marriage and family therapy and noticed that she and her husband seemed really happy together. Then I asked her if I could ask a few personal questions. She agreed.

"How long have you been married?" I began.

"About nineteen years," she replied.

"Have you always had such a loving and easy relationship?"

"Oh no, honey, we went through hell in the early years of our marriage and at several points since then. But we stuck it out. And it's paying off now."

Clearly, the couples I interviewed who appeared so satisfied with their marriages had gone through extremely difficult times. But something kept them together; some spark from heaven intervened and kept their passion for each other alive when the trials of life threatened to extinguish their love. Something inside of them recognized that breakthrough was just around the corner, and they took a deep breath and waited. They stuck together until that breakthrough burst through the turmoil of thoughts and wild imaginations of doom, and hope flooded in once again.

It helps if both husband and wife share the same faith and are attuned to the voice of the Lord correcting them, calling them to forgive one another and keeping their hearts soft and well oiled by the disciplines of prayer and worship.

Even in the best Christian marriages, however, the stressors of life and the stress of a spouse beginning to change into an unrecognizable person severely disrupt intimacy and undermine love.

In times like that, it is helpful to hear stories of how others handled such situations. We need to remember that God speaks to each person individually, and the wait to see if your partner actually heard the voice of God can be excruciating. It can be hard to give God time to work as He helps your spouse change and grow and learn to love in new ways.

During stressful times, we tend to react in one of two ways—either by drawing closer or by running away. Stress creates a fight-or-flight reaction. Fighting is fine—so long as you are fighting your own thoughts and not dishonoring the other or tearing him or her apart verbally. Fleeing is also a good idea—so long as you are fleeing to the arms of Jesus and talking it all over with Him. Most marriage partners survive the hard times by saying less and listening more. They thrive on a commitment to loving and honoring one another.

Many couples who are in ministry seem to have a particularly hard time. Not only do they have themselves to care for; they contend with the constant demands and overwhelming relational problems faced by a host of others. The stress is huge! And it threatens to undermine the most committed of couples. No matter if you and your spouse are in ministry or not, though, read on. All couples face circumstances they must work through together.

Here are a couple of stories from those in ministry who speak candidly about stressful situations that impacted their marriage. They moved suddenly from being depressed and visionless to being empowered and recommissioned. As you read their stories of fighting and fleeing, tuck their message away in your heart for a time when you might need it most. It is this:

## *Promise*

*Do not give up. You never know how close you are to breakthrough. God honors your commitment and covenant—in ministry and in marriage—and He will see you through.*

These couples experienced what the apostle Paul so often referred to—*stress* beyond our ability to cope. So what did Paul do? In 1 Timothy 1:12 he told us, "I thank Christ Jesus our Lord, who has given me strength, that he considered me faithful, appointing me to his service." Paul reminded himself of who he was—a man who once persecuted Jesus, and out of that, he became a man appointed by God to serve Him. Paul also reminded himself of who God is—the One who strengthened him in every dire circumstance. Paul was a man who learned the secret of being content and not letting discouragement and burnout keep him from finishing his race. Paul knew he was not a slave but was a son who had rightful access to the Father, who richly provides us with "everything we need for life and godliness" (2 Peter 1:3).

Paul also learned to access a secret weapon—the strength beyond his strength; the strength of God. His secret was this: "I can do everything through him who gives me strength" (Philippians 4:13). God honored Paul's commitment, as well as His own commitment to Paul. They worked together as friends bonded by bloodshed—not as master and servant trying to make up for past sins or gain favor for something more.

### Empowered and Recommissioned

Kim and Mary Andersson have weathered their share of storms in life. As the pastors of a small church in northern

153

California, their journey as a family and in ministry has not been an easy one. At one point, it seemed as though Kim and Mary were equally burned-out by life and ministry. Absolutely depleted, both felt unable to support and encourage one another, and both were left wondering, *Will our marriage survive? Will our ministry?*

Deeply committed to their marriage, Kim and Mary decided that if something was going to go—it would be the work of the ministry. It was too hard. They took a deep breath and drew away from one another for a brief season to fight the fight of resurrecting faith and to seek God's strength—in a sense, fleeing to God. And there, in that place of solitude, each listened for the promise of God, and God ignited the spark of hope and fanned the flames of strength once again. Mary tells the story:

> In our line of work as pastors, it's expected that we should display the supernatural on a regular basis; but as much as we need the supernatural realm in our public lives, we need it even more in our private world. We have the same needs, problems and personal issues as everyone in our congregation, but the majority of the time these needs must go on the back burner as we are called to care for others who may be in crisis. Days off and vacations are certainly a blessing, but the truth is, thoughts of those we care for are never far off, even while we are away. The minister's life is usually a life "on call."
>
> As ministers who both travel and pastor a local congregation, my husband and I have lives that are fully occupied with the needs of others. So as you can imagine, one of the great blessings in our "natural" world is the few close and true friends that we've come to know over the years. We share common vision, goals and interests as well as our "ups" and "downs" with this small group. When our schedules allow for time together, we laugh about nothing and everything. These folks are the ones whom we can enjoy unreservedly. They allow us to let our hair down and simply just be ourselves . . . the good,

154

the bad and the embarrassing, too. This band of friends called "ministers" can at times appear like an exclusive club, but in reality its members live such a unique and very public lifestyle . . . that these friendships could probably more adequately be compared to a "support" group than anything else!

When we were just beginning our church plant well over a decade ago, we were privileged to connect with another young couple who were pastoring a church on the other side of town. They enjoyed so many of the same things we did that it sometimes felt as though we were twins separated at birth . . . scary! We didn't often have time to be together, but our kids attended the same school, so we could grab little moments of fellowship as we came and went. School functions were the best, because we could actually have full conversations. One day we were at a school potluck, jabbering away, and our friends told us some news that they were immensely excited about but knew would be a huge blow to us. They shared that they were moving away.

I tried to choke back the tears as they were sharing about their new vision. I was sad that they were leaving . . . worried for my daughter who was best friends with their son. Besides the initial emotional reaction, I was truly happy for them; that they would not only be able to participate in the ministry of their dreams, but that they could now, after so many years, return to their hometown, where their extended family lived. They had been so homesick since they'd moved here. The husband was actually going to become a professor at the seminary he had graduated from, teaching and mentoring all the young pastors in training. The wife had also been hired by the college as the school chaplain. It was a marvelous opportunity for them. The open doors they were looking at were positively enviable!

As we drove home, I could barely speak. We had just come through a horrific year of church life, full of landfill-sized relational issues and replete with the stench of rejection. I just couldn't stop thinking about how nice it would be to teach full-time at a school that was training future ministers . . . those who were serious for the Lord and His purposes . . . wow, what could that look like? People who had actually paid cash money to hear you teach! And, besides that, to pastor only that crowd . . . what a piece of cake that would be. I had always loved the times in our many international travels when we would get the chance to speak at a Bible college. After all, I silently reasoned, Kim and I were college educated, and we had always related well to that age group and mindset . . . hmmm.

By the time we got home, I had entered into a complete blue funk, so I sat down on the couch to read for a little while, just to get away from my tortured thought life. We had a busy night of ministry ahead, so I really needed the break. At some point, I must have dozed off, and it was at that moment that the Lord decided to invade my sleep with a "God" dream. The dream was startlingly vivid, with smells and sights from the waking world. . . .

A father and son were driving down a country road together. As they traveled over hills that wound their way into the grazing lands of sheep and cows, the son began to pour out his soul to his dad. He had a captive audience, as his dad was trapped behind the steering wheel, traveling down a road that seemed to lead to no particular destination. Both father and son were from a long line of ministers . . . a multigenerational anointing. The son was in pastoral ministry and had become exceedingly weary with the load he was carrying. The father listened patiently as his son shared about the never-ending supply of people problems he had been sorting out. There were marriages falling apart, people backsliding, the sick and dying, the imprisoned and financially failing. And this was just the mundane, everyday list. Then there were the betrayers, the disloyal and the divisive to deal with. He was exhausted from his peace-keeping duties and wounded by the critical eyes that scrutinized him.

Dad just listened compassionately, with a deep concern that only a father knows. Then his son finally managed to circle his way to the real issue. He said, "Dad, I'm sorry, but

I'm done. I just can't take it anymore. I know this breaks your heart, but I can't be a pastor anymore . . . not another minute!" Without a word, his father suddenly swerved the car to the shoulder of the road, coming to a completely jarring halt. He nearly kicked the door open and went marching purposefully up the side of a nearby hill. *What's he up to?* wondered the son.

Dad slid under the fence and without missing a step headed directly for a small flock of sheep. The sheep instinctively knew to remain still, unruffled, as though they intimately knew this man. He rummaged around the lot of them till he located a small lamb, which he scooped up in his arms. Coming down the hill at the same pace he had ascended, when he got to the car, he pushed his way through the still-open door. He searched penetratingly into the eyes of his son as he thrust the young lamb into his arms. With the familiar voice from childhood that commands every son's attention, he said, "Feed my lambs!"

At precisely that moment, I bolted up from the couch and cried, "Yes, Father! I'm sorry!" Confused, I looked around the room. Noticing the clock, I realized that I had just sat down on the couch only twenty minutes prior to my startled awakening! The hand of the Lord had touched me and put me into a deep sleep for the express purpose of correcting my wayward course! In a moment's time, I went from depressed and visionless to empowered and recommissioned! This is why I'm fully convinced that we need the "super" to empower the "natural" parts of our lives. God is immensely practical and desires to intersect the places of our deepest felt needs. We were created for these times of encounter with God, and often, He desires to speak to us more than we're even able to listen! So He'll even "catch" us when we're asleep if He needs to!

It's so important for us to know our heavenly Father's heart and that He delights in sharing His secrets with us. Scripture tells us that Jesus only did what His Father told Him to do. We are really no different. It's absolutely essential for us to know what the Father has in mind for us. Because, you see, there is a vast difference between being a slave and a son. A slave never knows the plans of his master, only the tasks he's expected to do. He has no future, and no inheritance. However, a son will one day inherit everything his father owns, so when he is commissioned to do something for his father, he joyfully does it because he knows it will benefit the kingdom that also belongs to him. Ownership brings with it a deep and abiding sense of fulfillment and purpose. With the stresses of everyday life, I had forgotten my "daughter-ship" and had begun to act a bit more like a slave. What housewife hasn't felt that way on occasion?

In my spiritual encounter with the Lord that day, there were some significant truths that I needed to understand so that I wouldn't bow to the enemy of discouragement but instead be empowered for the rest of my journey. First of all, my perspective about my job was affecting my attitude. The enemy had succeeded in making me feel like a failure. But the Lord wanted me to see that I was His daughter, that I had a generational inheritance that came from Him and that it wasn't simply a "job," but it was really a gift from His hand. The truth is, as long as any of us continue to do what He tells us to do, we are not failures!

Truth is . . . I almost gave up! Then I would never have seen the rewards of following God's agenda for our lives. In the ensuing years, we've seen thousands of lives delivered, healed and restored for the Kingdom. We've traveled to many nations and have even seen our own children participate in the blessings of what we've been allowed to "plant" for the Lord. One of our sons recently received a full scholarship from a Bible college that we've ministered to frequently over the last decade. What a tragedy it would have been to miss that blessing. There is no greater fulfillment in life than to enjoy what is on God's heart for us to do. His purposes for our lives (even when they appear to our eyes as dull or mundane) have a ripple effect for eternity.

I encourage you to allow the Lord to penetrate your everyday life with a renewed perspective. Embrace His plans for you, by embracing the "right now" of your life. Ask Him to catch you while you're sleeping, so you can "rediscover" your passion, as I did![1]

## Adapting to a Changing Spouse

Michal Ann and James Goll had been in ministry for many years, trapped in the cultural religiosity of their day and their church culture. Then they experienced a season of divine intervention that shook their theology and transformed the dynamics of their marriage and ministry. But every couple knows that when one partner changes the dance, you begin to step on each other's toes. A changing spouse is difficult for many men and women to accept and threatens the equilibrium and established roles. Crisis ensues! It is during those seasons that a marriage must adapt to change or break down. Here is Michal Ann's story:[2]

Beginning on the Day of Atonement in 1992—on October 6—our family entered a nine-week period of visitation encounters that forever changed our lives, especially mine. In retrospect, I suppose that period was a compressed "pregnancy" in the spirit realm, but one measured in weeks instead of months. By the time my "pregnancy" was over, God had birthed in me a whole new identity that literally changed my relationship with Jim and revolutionized our approach to ministry.

On that October night in 1992, I had no idea that I was about to have an extraordinary experience. Like millions of other busy parents across the world, I had struggled with my kids during the day and couldn't wait to get them in bed so I could get some rest. I had prayed some of the same prayers you have probably prayed: "Lord, I want to see You, I want to know You, and I want to have encounters with You. Help me, God!" I had no clue how seriously God took my simple prayer.

Although I had walked closely with God from my childhood, I, like many of you, needed to rediscover personal "ownership" in my relationship with Him. Before I met Jim, I had a very strong walk with Jesus, whom I considered my best friend. After Jim and I married, I overreacted to his strong revelatory gifts and ministry anointing. Unconsciously, I began to ride on his spiritual coattails. At times, if I needed to hear from God, I let Jim do the listening for me. Eventually, I put more trust in what Jim said the Lord was saying than in my own perception of what He was saying. The Holy Spirit's voice gradually became faint to my ears.

Then the Lord began convicting me of this imbalance in my life. Tied into the problem was my deep desire to escape the bondage of intimidation and the fear of man. I dreamed of the day when I would be brave enough to step out and take a gamble for God.

Jim's class ran late that night, and afterward he drove home our good friend Chris Berglund. Chris was Jim's teaching assistant that year. As they drove, Jim felt his left ear suddenly pop open. Just before Chris got out of the car, Jim turned to him and said, "Chris, God is going to speak tonight." Jim later told me, "I had no idea what I was saying, but I knew an encounter was on the way. Little did I know the magnitude and effect of the invasion that was about to come into our lives."

A short time later, Jim suddenly awoke and sat up in bed. He glanced at the clock (Jim's years of prayer and prophetic ministry had conditioned him to look at our digital clock to check the time whenever he woke up). The clock read 11:59 P.M.—one minute before midnight on the Day of Atonement.

Earlier that night, our third child, Tyler, had joined me in the bedroom because he was frightened by the storm. Now, he lay sound asleep on the floor by Jim's side of the bed. Jim had been startled awake when a lightning bolt crashed down in our backyard and seemed to come right through the bedroom window. Tyler slept through the whole event, and so did I!

In the flickering glow of that lightning strike, without any prior warning, Jim suddenly saw a man standing in our room, and this angel was looking straight at him! This stare went on for what Jim still calls "the longest minute of my life." Then, a ball of white light came in and hovered like a spotlight over a letter on my dresser. The letter was from a prophetic friend

160

from New York City named David. It contained a prophetic word, along with some pictures that he had drawn of what he called "an old-fashioned swashbuckler" with a sharp sword. David believed this to be a prophetic picture of the authority God had given us to minister deliverance to those in bondage. For five hours, the ball of light remained in a fixed position over that letter on my dresser.

Jim describes his experience that night as follows:

> *I was shaking in the presence of God. That room was filled with what I can only describe as "the terror of God." I'm not talking about some nice, gentle little fear of God—this was absolutely frightening. It wasn't the first time I'd experienced that kind of terror of God, though. I had encountered it two times before, but each time I knew that I was in the holy, manifested presence of God. On this particular night, I felt as though I was about to crawl out of my skin.*
>
> *This man looked at me, and I looked at him, but neither one of us said anything. When the clock turned to midnight, I heard an audible voice say, "Watch your wife. I am about to speak to her." Right after that, the man (I believe he was an angel) disappeared—but the terror of the Lord remained in our room. As soon as the angel disappeared, Michal Ann woke up.*

When I woke up, Jim turned to me and whispered, "Ann, an angel has just come." He was trembling, and suddenly I knew why. Jim didn't bother to tell me that his left ear had opened up, or that he had told Chris that God was going to speak that night. He didn't even tell me what the angel had said, or what he looked like. (Jim later described the angel as having the appearance of a man dressed in brown and wearing trousers and shoes. He thought the angel might have been some sort of servant messenger.)

We had been through enough past experiences for me to know that when Jim whispered "Ann!" the way he did that night, a major occurrence was happening. I immediately thought, *Oh no, it's happening again!* I was really scared, but I also knew that we were in the midst of an extraordinarily wonderful moment. No one describes such an experience better than the venerable Job:

> *Now a thing was secretly brought to me,*
> *and my ear received a whisper of it.*
> *In thoughts from the visions of the night,*
> *when deep sleep falls on men,*
> *Fear came upon me and trembling, which*
> *made all my bones shake.*
> *Then a spirit passed before my face; the*
> *hair of my flesh stood up!*
>
> Job 4:12–15, AMP

The moment I woke up, I also felt the terror of the Lord present in the room. No pile of covers was high enough to shield me from His presence. At that moment, I just wanted to crawl to the foot of my bed with about twenty covers over me, but I knew I would still feel as if covered only by a thin, little sheet. Amazingly, little Tyler continued to sleep soundly through the entire event, but Jim and I literally shook under the covers for half an hour. Then, to my amazement, my dear husband rolled over and fell asleep! To this day, I have never been able to understand how he could do that! Between shakes I thought, *How could he leave me alone like this? The least he could do was stay with me, so we could go through this together.* But instead, he went to sleep.

So there I was, lying awake and shaking in fear under the covers. I thought, *Okay, this is an opportunity from the Lord for me to be bold, and go for everything that the Lord has for me.* So I began to cry out to God, "Lord, I want to know what You are doing. I want to hear what You are saying. I invite Your presence; I invite Your Holy Spirit. Everything that You want to do, I want You to do it. I am

162

just presenting myself here before You." I was putting my best foot forward in the only way I knew how.

The terror of His presence permeated the room. I was still shaking, and all I could do was wait and see what the Lord might do. For the past three days, I had suffered with severe earaches caused by exposure to cold weather and wind. My ears were hurting that night, so I was lying on my stomach with one ear on the pillow. Suddenly, I felt liquid warmth, like that of oil, flowing into my exposed ear—it was very soothing. I was being healed.

Although still nearly paralyzed with fear, I decided to try a big experiment. That warm oil in my exposed ear felt so good that I very carefully, and slowly, turned my head to expose the other ear. What would happen? Would I cut off the anointing of God and offend Him? I didn't want to make any wrong move that might cause His presence to leave! As soon as I turned my head, the warm oil began to pour into my other ear. That's when everything suddenly began to change.

I had been lying there for about ninety minutes, just waiting on the Lord. I turned to look at the clock, which now read 1:34 in the morning. That time was a significant signpost. I didn't know it at that point, but Psalm 134:1 signified what the Lord was going to have me do for the next nine weeks: "Behold, bless the LORD, all servants of the LORD, who serve by night in the house of the LORD!" (NASB).

After this, what I first noticed was feeling pressure building up in my head, and it quickly became very intense, to the point where I was almost ready to scream. At the very moment when I thought I couldn't handle it anymore, the pressure moved from my head to my back. It felt as if someone had laid a board across my back—right along my spine—and was literally trying to push the breath out of my body! Desperately, I tried to reach out to Jim, but something was holding my hand back. I felt my body literally being moved away from him, while, at the same time, the pressure against my back was pressing everything out of me. I came out of this experience feeling as though I didn't even know what I looked like anymore.

Was I still alive? I actually put my fingers on my throat and checked my pulse to make sure. What had happened to me? I felt as if I had just undergone major internal surgery. I even got up, went into the bathroom and looked in the mirror to see if my hair had turned white or if my face appeared different. I had no doubt that the Holy Spirit had performed some sort of radical deliverance on me, but I still had no idea what exactly He had done.

After this ordeal, we asked the Lord to confirm these experiences through our children, if they were from Him. When little Tyler woke up later that morning, without prompting, he stood right up and announced his dream that angels had visited our house. Our oldest son, who was upstairs in bed that night, also told us his detailed dream about a winged white horse!

At 2:04 A.M., Jim suddenly woke up again and asked me what was happening. He could sense that the Lord's awesome presence was still in the room. I already found it difficult to talk. Every time I tried, I could feel the "waves" of His presence increase even more in intensity and power. This was most apparent in moments when I became too close to the crucial part of my experiences over the past few hours. At those times, the fear of the Lord was so great that I simply couldn't talk. This visitation left both Jim and me shaking in bed. We would rest for twenty minutes of trembling, and, when we felt the intensity begin to subside a little, we would begin to talk and pray again. Sure enough, another wave would come into the room and engulf us. God was trying to tell us something! Meanwhile, we noticed the glowing light still hovering over near the dresser—even though the thunderstorm had passed and all the lightning was gone! Waves of God's presence continued to flow over me through the night.

When morning finally arrived, Jim got up and left me in bed. When I finally got up, I was still jumpy; I was so totally submerged in the supernatural realm that simple acts like making breakfast were beyond me. I could not fix my daughter's hair or help my children get ready for school; I just was not operating on a practical plane. I remember sitting on the couch—with my face turned away from all the activity going on—when one of my children came up behind me and tapped me on the shoulder. I suddenly jumped and looked around as if to say, "Who are you? Oh, you're my son." I was expecting another surprise visitor from the heavenly realm.

Later that morning, I called our intercessory friend Pat Gastineau of Atlanta, Georgia. The Holy Spirit indicated that Pat would have discernment on some of the previous night's events. She shared her perceptions, which I found quite helpful. Pat interpreted the pressure I experienced on my back as God's tool for driving fear and unbelief out of my life. My encounter seemed to be a picture of what He desires the Church to experience. Thank God for our friends! I have to say that Jim was very gracious, and my kids were very understanding during the next nine weeks. My family got a taste of life without regular "Mom-cooked" meals, and without any practical activities that moms do, such as housecleaning.

The very next night, God's presence again entered our bedroom at about 2 A.M. and began to minister to me (while Jim continued to sleep). This pattern repeated almost every night for nearly nine weeks. Most nights, the Lord's presence came so strongly that I feared that I might not live through the experience. On many nights, particularly when Jim was away on a ministry trip, I would stay up far into the morning hours. I had no idea what sort of experience I would be walking into.

I know that linking words like *fear* and *terror* with the God of love, grace and mercy may sound strange. But remember that when God comes to us in intimate communion, He comes to take over. For mortal men and women, that can be a frightening experience. Just examine all the instances when God or messengers appeared to mortals in Scripture. In virtually every instance, the first words said to the humans were "Fear not" or "Peace." There is a reason!

Jim and I were both overwhelmed by the magnitude of the changes that resulted from these visitations. Several discussions included statements from him such as, "Michal, you're not like you used to be—you're not the same person I married."

Then I would deliver a very uncharacteristic reply such as, "You didn't expect me to stay the same, did you? Didn't you expect me to grow and to change?" So we went back and forth, as do other married couples who are trying to rework and readjust their relationship to accommodate change. We had to reexamine every aspect of how we treated each other. We realized that we had to allow, and even encourage, each other to come into everything the Lord had for us. That meant having to remove every "nice" controlling factor, such as that statement, "But I like you just the way you are." The proper answer (given in love, of course) was, "Well, honey, if I'm getting closer to God, then you'll like me even more. You can't lose."

> We realized that we had to allow, and even encourage, each other to come into everything the Lord had for us.

Jim and I discovered that we could no longer assume that we understood what the other person was saying or thinking. We had to step back and become reacquainted with ourselves. Old, overly familiar statements like, "Oh yeah, I know what you mean," wouldn't do anymore. Once we realized that God was changing our personal walk with Him, and our marriage relationship, we felt the Lord's comfort. The Bible says, "Can two walk together, except they be agreed?" (Amos 3:3, KJV). We had come into a new place of agreement: Neither one of us knew what I was changing into! As odd as it sounds, this gave us some common ground to work from. We made a commitment to walk with each other through change. This huge issue dealt with commitment and covenant, and it also stretched our communication skills.

As I prayed about these experiences—and spoke with other people more seasoned in walking with God—I began to realize that Jim and I had been exposed to "the jealousy of God." The Lord spoke to him about me and said, "Before she was ever yours, she was Mine."

That is true for every one of us! Before we ever belonged to anyone else, we were His first, and He will always maintain first rights to us as His beloved. God is a jealous Lord of us as His priests and His holy people. As Jim often explains in our meetings, "I actually had to call home to find out what God was saying during those nine weeks. I was no longer just married to this wonderfully sweet woman and mother of our four children. Now, I was married to an anointed woman of God!"

Under these new circumstances, we had to relearn how to relate to each other. In Jim's words, I was now "possessed by God." Encounters with heaven will always create adjustments on earth. Be warned. Be blessed. And ask for more! His grace is always sufficient to carry us through the transitions.[3]

God honors commitment and covenant—in ministry and in marriage. "Those who honor me I will honor," He tells us in 1 Samuel 2:30. That is His promise, and honoring you will be His provision, revealed in ways that you may not immediately recognize. His Word focuses on covenants and commitments and promises strength to see us through. As you release honor to one another, honor will come to you. As you honor the Lord by seeking Him for strength to follow through on your commitments, He will honor you with grace and strength. When life changes and the stress of marriage or ministry threatens to overwhelm you, set your focus on God. You may not be able to change your spouse or your circumstances, but His grace, wisdom, redirection, strategy and strength are yours for the asking.

# 9

# STUMBLING INTO DESTINY

"You are so much more than you have become," declared the Lion King to his young son in the Disney film *The Lion King*. And so it is with all of us. In my work as a counselor and teacher, I have heard people of all ages express a longing to capture that passion of youth that says, "I will be somebody!"

Some of us are a little slower than others to catch hold of our lives and focus in on the purpose and calling that leads us to become who God intended us to be all along. Eventually, we discover where our interests, gifts and talents emerge, and we begin to shape a life for ourselves. Eventually, we may even stumble into our destiny. My journey speaks to the slow, circuitous route of stumbling toward destiny. And it also speaks to the grace of God. He positions us for purpose and orchestrates the divine appointments we need to encourage us onto the right path. He even occasionally speeds up the journey. He also reveals to us, at every age and season in our lives, that we are so much more than we have become. We are children of the Lion King—born to rule and reign on this side of heaven and in the age to come.

What happens when you lose sight of who you are and where you are going? The gracious nature of God comes alongside and says, "This is the way. Walk in it." God ensures that we do not miss it.

I always knew that I was called to be a writer. Throughout my school years, I spent more time reading novels and writing short stories than I did on homework. In college, I loved my creative writing professors, and they loved my work. However, I felt that I needed to major in something that would help me earn a living. After all, writers and artists have a reputation for being poor. So I majored in journalism and went to work as a newspaper reporter and editor. Before long, it became evident that I would rather write long feature stories than short news reports on politics, school board shenanigans and obituaries. And it was not long before I woke up to the fact that I could make more money if I dumped newspaper work and switched careers. So I used my writing ability in public relations and marketing. But I was unhappy. Something in me kept whispering, "You are so much more than you have become."

I wrote a book on teen pregnancy, using my journalistic skills to interview different young women about their unplanned pregnancies and the repercussions of the choices they had made. By the age of thirty, I had a book published with a major Christian publisher—*The Note on the Mirror: Pregnant Teens Tell Their Stories* (Zondervan, 1990). It was a step closer to where God would encourage me to go later in life, but I was young and not listening to the Lion King. Not long after the book came out, I decided to return to school for a master's degree in family counseling. Once there, my professors often commented on my writing ability after they read the papers I turned in. Was I a writer? Or a counselor? Was I both? I worked in the counseling field for many years, but still, something whispered deep in my heart that I was so much more than I had become.

Years later, after losing the funding for my job as a school counselor, I decided to take a month or so and do what I had always dreamed of doing—going off and writing a novel. So I went to Kona, Hawaii, and spent two months caught up in the joy of creating. I felt God's pleasure as I wrote. Little did I know that God had decided to set me up with a divine appointment that would enable me to stumble into my destiny.

It was there, at a little church in Kona, that I met a British man named David Aikman. He had been one of our heroes in the journalism field when I was in college. Former *Time* magazine bureau chief in Beijing and Jerusalem, he had focused his recent years on writing for Christian magazines, publishing books and putting together a PBS series about famous world Christians. He also authored historical works, including one that spoke about the history of Christianity in China and where the Chinese house church movement was going. As a result of his work in China, David was now working on congressional hearings about the plight of Chinese Christians. His career had evolved from being a journalist to becoming a Christian statesman.

As David told me the story of his journey, I realized that we are all stumbling toward our destiny. Destiny changes. Who we are and what we do at different points in our lives will eventually converge into something so much more than we ever thought that we would become. But the key is to stay close to the heartbeat of the Father and position ourselves for purpose.

Meeting David Aikman so inspired me that I decided my

Destiny changes. Who we are and what we do at different points in our lives will eventually converge into something so much more than we ever thought that we would become.

first love was indeed writing and that I needed to get back into writing for Christian publications. So I resumed my calling as a writer. I started writing profiles of Christian leaders for *Charisma* magazine. After writing about Bill Johnson, Mahesh Chavda, John Sandford and a few others, it dawned on me that God was taking me somewhere with all this writing. But where? I began asking God for the spirit of wisdom and revelation, for His strategy. I wanted to know what was in His dream for me, and I wanted to start dreaming bigger with Him.

Over the years, I had tucked away many ideas for books in my files. One book series kept nagging at me, and I knew the time had come to write it. But who would publish it? I had no reputation as an author. Neither did I have a big platform for book sales. Worse yet, the books I wanted to write were not girlie books, as many series are. They would be written for leaders in the Church. I figured that no publisher would touch me, so I sought the Lord in prayer. His promise came quickly.

---

### Promise

*With God all things are possible.*

Matthew 19:26

---

The key words that leapt off the page were "with God." How do I work with God? God had already rekindled the desire in me to write books that would build up the Church and inspire readers to enter into God encounters and move into their spiritual callings. He set me up to meet David Aikman and other Christian leaders. He could and would move mountains and open doors for me. He was clearly working on my behalf, but I wondered how to work *with* Him. Then the Holy Spirit spoke to my heart, *Seek the Lord for the strategy.*

Of course! So many leaders in the Old Testament sought the Lord, or inquired of the Lord, during times of battle that I decided to do the same. It was time to stop stumbling around in my own head and begin to inquire of the Lord.

His answer came quickly. *Ask those you have written about to contribute chapters.*

Brilliant idea! So I asked Graham Cooke if he would write the foreword to my first book, *Shifting Shadows of Supernatural Power* (Destiny Image, 2006), and he agreed. I dropped his name to the acquisitions editor of a publishing house, and the editor responded right away—he was interested! I then asked Bill Johnson and Mahesh Chavda if they would contribute chapters to the book. They readily agreed. I could not believe it. The project came together very quickly and became a success.

The second book in the series, *Shifting Shadows of Supernatural Experiences* (Destiny Image, 2007), followed, with James Goll as the coauthor. In that book, we wrote about the variety of spiritual experiences and how to discern what may be from God, what may have originated in yourself and what may be a demonic counterfeit. Suddenly, I realized that my journalism and counseling backgrounds and training were converging in this book. God uses all of our experiences in life to position us for purpose. It is only in midlife, I believe, that we begin to see our gifts and talents converge into a sense of satisfaction that we have indeed become so much more than we ever dreamed or imagined.

Now that I was beginning to build a readership and some name recognition, it was time to fly on my own as an author. I started self-publishing a few of my books and speaking at women's retreats and writers' conferences, and occasionally in churches. I felt as though I was no longer stumbling toward my destiny—I was soaring into it! And as I give myself to the creative process, I lose

God uses all of our experiences in life to position us for purpose.

my fear of not being able to make a living. I have been in a long transition process of letting go of my counseling employment to focus on giving myself solely to writing and publishing, but I am getting closer. And I am enjoying life more.

We are all stumbling toward some destiny in life. What is your destiny? Are there hopes and dreams you may have left by the roadside out of fear, thinking you could not earn a living that way or wondering what your family and friends might think? If God is whispering to you that you are so much more than you have become, when are you going to get on with the journey?

## Working with God

God is the God of strategy and big ideas. When we seek to work with God, moments of divine inspiration suddenly crash into our awareness. God gives an idea, but we must walk it out. I walked out the book publishing strategy by summoning my courage to ask others to contribute chapters. Inventors also summon the courage to ask for investors. I have heard of people young and old acting on an idea God gave them and making great money in the process. One young man created a cross of nails and received so many comments on it that he decided to mass-produce them and sell them during a week-long Christian rock concert. His idea paid off handsomely. Another man, an ophthalmologist in the Virginia Beach area, received an idea for laser surgery that would restore the eyesight of thousands of people. His patent enabled him to live comfortably and retire young, and it seemed as if he had reached the pinnacle of his destiny and blessed masses of people in the process. Rather than relax and retire, however, he lives humbly and spends his time doing medical missions in foreign countries.

When we work with God, we receive heaven's strategies. Doors to divine appointments open where we receive the equipment or the funding that we need to go ahead with an idea God has given us. Yet there are other times when we need to learn that working with God means not running ahead of Him. The Bible is full of stories in which God spoke specific direction to individuals and even barred their way when He wanted to redirect them for some reason. The apostle Paul received much personal direction—sometimes through angels, often just out of his personal relationship with Jesus. Paul learned to discern His voice over the years and let God direct—or redirect—his course.

Some incidents in the Bible are about God telling someone not to continue in the direction they had set their minds to. It is important to listen if God steers us in a different direction from the one we are headed in, yet God still speaks to us individually—if we are listening.

## When Doors Slam Shut

Faith listens and waits for God, as missionaries Ron and Suzanne Keitzer learned:

"Look, honey! Korean Air is offering really cheap airfare to Manila! We can fly from there to that TESOL class (Teachers of English to Speakers of Other Languages) on that southern island that is so much less expensive than the one here," Suzanne Keitzer said to her husband, Ron, one morning. She was excited about the opportunity to take a class in the field where they could put into immediate practice what they would learn by reaching Muslim students on a Philippine island. He agreed, and off she rushed to the computer to book the airline tickets.

Within moments of trying to input the flight data and book the tickets online, her computer screen suddenly went haywire and erased her data. She called a travel agent at Priceline, and as he tried to input the information, his frustrated voice replied that his computer screen was going haywire as well. He told her to wait so he could call the airlines directly.

Meanwhile, she began praying. "Lord, if You are trying to block the way, please make it really clear. So clear that I don't miss it."

The agent came back on the line and said apologetically that Korean Air had decided to cancel the very flight she wanted. She would have to take a flight leaving a day later and pay a great deal more.

With a heavy heart, Suzanne hung up the phone and began asking God why she could not go when she felt that their calling, now that they had retired, was to teach English as a second language. "Why did You block the way, Lord?" she asked. "I really wanted to go!"

Weeks later, God revealed His reasons for making them stay home. By then, the Keitzers had left their home in Tucson, Arizona, and were volunteering at a state park, working in the visitors center near Las Cruces, New Mexico. On their way in to work, they stopped for a cup of coffee. Out of habit, Ron reached for the newspaper at hand. What he read sent shivers down his spine. Silently, he pushed the newspaper to his wife and pointed out the headline about Manila.

During the week they would have been on the island, the news reported that extremist rebels were rampaging for political control not 25 miles from where they would have been. They were taking hostages and making international news. Their target? Missionaries and teachers.

Thankful that God had spared their lives, Suzanne could not believe the next bit of news her husband pulled from the paper later that week. Apparently, the flight that she had considered booking on another airline had crashed into the sea, killing all aboard. Two near misses. Apparently when God slams a door shut, His intentions may yet be to enable you to fulfill your calling and reach your destiny. Good thing she had listened and had not tried to force the door open another way.

"God had given us the desire to teach, and we never questioned it. But the timing and place for our training was on hold for a little while," Suzanne said, noting that

God ultimately helps us fulfill His plans and purposes for us. Within the year, God had provided the funds for them to study TESOL in Kona, Hawaii. Today they serve as missionaries, teaching English as a second language to foreign students studying in the United States.

Sometimes you need to lay down the dream for a season. If it is God, He will release it to you in His time and in His way. Then there are times when God calls you to give away the very thing that you need in order to move into your calling or reach your destiny. It is as if He is saying, "Yes, I want you to travel north, but take a little detour south first."

Why would God prompt someone to move in the opposite direction from where he or she needs to end up? When doors slam shut, perhaps it happens so we can learn to trust in His provision and in His ability to redirect us to where we need to go. We can do much in our own strength to establish our lives, but in God's strength, we become established in His life. We learn that God often

We can do much in our own strength to establish our lives, but in God's strength, we become established in His life.

moves in the opposite spirit of our culture. We think we need to acquire things to help us on the journey of life. God's economy states something entirely different: If you want to receive, learn to give it all away. If you want to learn to trust God, hear and obey. If you want to receive something that you believe you need, give what you have away.

## Magical Thinking versus Faith

Sometimes, we think that because God has spoken a clear direction, it is time to jump up and get moving. The doors seem to be open, and we want to rush through them. We want to run into our destiny before it is time. But it takes time to become so much more than who we already are. We have so much more to learn and to give one another along the journey.

Quite often, people come up to me during writers' conferences and ask for an impartation of the ability to write. They believe that if I would only lay my hands on their heads, they would suddenly discover an amazing gift of writing flowing from them, which would then cause the doors of publishing houses to fly open. Their magical thinking is born of a desire to shortcut the process of learning the writing craft, as if destiny is something you walk into easily. However, it takes faith to develop your gifting and press on into your calling. Even gifts must be exercised, honed into a fine edge and developed into a skill. Jesus was not born a carpenter. He became one. I was not born a writer. I became one. The gifts lie dormant until you pick up the tools of your craft and begin to use them.

People often think that defining their destiny and calling is the difficult part, and that once they do so, reaching the desired outcome is a given. It is true that reaching your destiny is a process dependent on God, not a destination you achieve in your own strength and time, but magical thinking will not get you there. Faith combined with action will. Have faith in the Holy Spirit's ability to guide and release favor, and then step out in faith to do the work God requires of you. There are no shortcuts.

I listened to two ministry school students talking in a hallway one day. The first student was despondent because she did not have the funds to continue school or pay the rent that was a week overdue. She was coming to the sad conclusion that it was time to leave school, move back home and get a job. The second student tried to encourage her by saying that God had led them there and that He would provide. He proceeded to tell her recent stories of how God had provided money for school and rent for many students. But the first student seemed more interested in whining than in working and trusting.

As I listened to them, I realized that the first student had come to school with one thought in mind—"I want this! It must be God's will! Let others pay my way." She had no desire to get a job and pay her own way. Neither did she intend to go into ministry. She just wanted to move out of her parents' house and be entertained among other students—right in the middle of the action. Her magical thinking led to great disappointment.

The second student had waited and said, "I believe this is God's will. Because of the promise and nudge that He gave me, I can trust that He will provide for my every need or give me the strategy and jobs that I need to fund this endeavor." His faith led to a deeper encounter with God.

Magical thinking says, "I want this, so my Father must want it for me!" It is born of a demanding spirit, full of self-will, ignorant of God's will. It evades responsibility. It wants to escape from the conditions God has established in order for a person to exercise his or her gifts and take steps of faith on a daily basis. It causes one to move in presumption rather than seek God's will and timing. It acts with a sense of entitlement to a specific outcome. It gives up when the process seems too long. Those who move in magical thinking usually have no depth of relationship with God—they know nothing of His ways and little about His character. It is an immature, childish faith.

Faith, on the other hand, appropriates the promises of the Father as His Word leaps into your heart. It partners with God's will, turning it back to Him in prayer, with thanksgiving. It assumes responsibility to meet certain conditions to achieve the desired outcome. Faith surrenders to the process rather than demanding that the outcome look a certain way or arrive at a certain time. Those who move in faith tend to be friends with God—they care about His plans and purposes, and they experience a depth to their relationship that enables them to trust the nature of God.

Faith comes to understand that when we take a long detour on our journey, God will ultimately intervene and redirect us . . . if we let Him. Faith also knows that doors to fulfilling our calling or destiny—doors of favor that we think should swing wide open—often slam shut. Yet if we wait, His purposes often become evident. If we act presumptuously and try to make our own way past the shut doors, disaster may curtail all our best intentions. Faith waits for God. Faith holds onto promises and prophecies, so that a person moves toward the goal with God rather than operating in his or her own strength and strategy.

## Waiting on God

Faith waits on God, but waiting is not about sitting down passively, hoping God will move. Waiting is an action verb. You can have faith that what God has spoken to you personally will come to pass, but you must add something to the waiting: You must engage in a process of prayer, remembering and declaring the promises of God, asking Him for more power and revelation and favor. You must position yourself in a place of continual dependency on the grace of God.

Bill Johnson, pastor of Bethel Church in Redding, California, exemplifies a man who has increased in favor through the years as he has waited on God for more power in his ministry—power to build up the Body of Christ and motivate an army of revivalists who will impact every mountain of influence in the world. He carried the personal words of destiny deep in his heart and prayed and declared the goodness of God faithfully for decades. As a result, his ministry flourished, and his church shifted from experiencing moments of revival to years of continuous revival.

Bill knew, however, that God had so much more to do through him—beyond Redding and into the nations. So he kept waiting. He did not run ahead of himself into self-promotion or encourage viral hype through the Internet about what was transpiring in his church in Redding. He kept waiting, asking for more of God. He did not try to move in his own power or manipulate events in his church. He kept waiting and praying for more of God, *at any cost*. And one night, the moment came when he knew that God was empowering him for the next level of ministry.

In 1995, in the middle of the night, God came in answer to Bill's prayer of "I must have more of You at any cost!" Here is Bill's account of the moment when he knew God was answering that prayer and positioning him for more favor:

I went from a dead sleep to being wide-awake in a moment. Unexplainable power began to pulsate through my body, seemingly just shy of electrocution. It was as though I had been plugged into a light socket with a thousand volts of electricity flowing through my body. My arms and legs shot out in silent explosions as if something was released through my hands and my feet. The more I tried to stop it, the worse it got. . . . The divine moment was glorious, but not pleasant.[1]

Bill felt so unable to control his muscle responses during the encounter that he envisioned having spastic muscle contractions, his arms and legs flailing out of control in front of his church or on the street, people stopping to stare at him as if he had physical problems—a most undignified situation. He was not sure he would ever be able to function as a normal human being again—it felt as though he had completely lost the capacity to use his body normally. He continues:

At the forefront was the realization that God wanted to make an exchange—His increased presence for my dignity. It's

181

difficult to explain how you know the purpose of such an encounter. You just know. You know His purpose so clearly that every other reality fades into the shadows, as God puts His finger on the one thing that matters to Him.[2]

I asked Bill to elaborate on the encounter, and this is what he replied: "When I said 'I'll gladly make the exchange,' it was because I thought I might be bedridden the rest of my life—and that it was okay with me if I got God's manifest presence in the exchange. He could do anything He wanted to me if I got more of Him."

Since that time, Bill Johnson has had ongoing experiences of the electrifying empowerment of God, and as a result, he has gained an international reputation as a healing revivalist who is mobilizing the Body of Christ to transform communities and nations in the naturally supernatural power of God.[3]

Receiving God's promise and provision to reach our destinies involves working with Him, acting in faith and waiting for more of the power of God. Those whose stories I have told here are moving straight into their destinies and accessing the power and revelation they need for business and ministry, through faith. They realize that faith is a never-ending cycle, and they begin each day with seeking the Lord and end each day with worshiping and blessing the Lord.

Who knows the day or the hour when God will visit you and empower you for the next level, shifting you from provision for the task at hand into great prosperity? What do you need? Power to minister to others? God's presence to come and comfort you during a dark night of the soul? A change in your circumstances? Something added to your life? Whatever you need, wait for Him. Ask for Him. He will surely come!

And when He does, He likely will put His finger on something in your life, as He did in Bill's life. You may need to give something up, as Bill gave up his dignity, or you may need to give something away. Willingness to give seems to be the main condition of becoming prosperous.

## The Conditions of Prosperity

Give, and it will be given to you. A good measure, pressed down, shaken together and running over, will be poured into your lap. For with the measure you use, it will be measured to you.

Luke 6:38

During the 70s and 80s, new mission movements were launching thousands into the world with nothing but a Bible and faith in God's miraculous provision and protection coming when they needed it. Testimonies abounded about how people would smuggle Bibles past border patrols in communist countries, the eyes of the guards somehow not seeing the boxes of contraband literature despite staring straight at them. Other mission stories spoke of food or medicine arriving at just the right moment or an escape route opening up. God always came through.

One organization, Youth With A Mission (YWAM), has a long history of testimonies of God's provision. YWAM still teaches its students how to live by faith. And their stories still inspire me with the knowledge that God will always make a way—in His time. And as we learn to give, we receive so much more than we ever dreamed.

One young mother of two children worked with her husband at a YWAM base in Amsterdam. They reached out to those working in the red light district and to the hordes of wandering youth that shifted through the city during the summers. One day as she sat in church, she felt the Lord prompting her to give all that she had in the offering. She counted out her money and it came to $15, just what she needed for groceries to feed her children. She had no other money, and none was expected to arrive in the near future. What does a mother do? Give to the Lord or provide for her children? The urge to give was so strong that she decided to drop the money into the offering quickly, before she changed her mind.

"What now, God? What was that about?" she asked as she left the church.

Before she had walked two blocks toward home, a woman walked up to her with two grocery bags in her arms and said, "Here! I thought you could use these." She gave them to the young mother and walked away.

The reply of the Lord came to her, *Give and it will be given to you abundantly.*

It was a lesson in faith—not in her ability to provide for herself and her family, but in God's willingness to care for them all in ways far beyond their comprehension. When we meet the needs of others, God rushes in to provide for us.

During a Patricia King conference, I witnessed an extraordinary exercise in learning to give away what you think you need to reach your destiny. Patricia had spent years with YWAM when her family was young, and throughout those years she and her husband had learned that when God promises something, He makes good on His word. They had learned to live by faith in His faithfulness.

Now an internationally known minister and a hip and trendy grandmother with a ministry based in Phoenix, Arizona, Patricia hosted a conference called God's Media Army a few years ago.[4] Many people who worked in the movie industry attended that conference. Most were struggling producers, writers and students. Everyone arrived with a creative dream, and everyone longed for some inspiration or divine provision that would catapult them into reaching their destiny—or at least get their projects one step further down the road.

Patricia embodies faith in action. And she models what she has learned throughout every conference she hosts. During one session, she pointed to a young woman and asked her to stand up. "What is your dream? What do you want to do?" she asked the girl.

"I want to be a photographer, but I have only a little digital camera and no money to buy better equipment or to attend school," she replied hesitantly.

The word *but* does not seem to exist in Patricia's vocabulary. It only seems to rile her up.

"You want to be a photographer but only have a little camera. Why don't you give that camera away and watch what God gives you in return? If you give, it will be given to you in a greater measure than ever before," she told the girl.

Immediately, the girl turned to face the audience and shouted, "Who needs this camera more than I do?"

A few hands went into the air, including a young boy. The girl ran over to the boy and gave the camera to him, to encourage him toward his desire to become a photographer. And then she sat down in the midst of thunderous applause.

Suddenly, a man stood up and walked over to the girl. He held out a large camera bag. Inside was a professional-quality digital camera with several lenses. He gave it to the girl and said that he and his wife had a photography studio and school and that she was welcome to come and learn the art of photography for free.

Patricia then asked who else needed something to help them fulfill their dream. A couple stood and said that they needed some really expensive movie cameras to finish a film they were working on. They had brought along one professional camera worth several thousand dollars, but it was not good enough to meet their needs.

Patricia just smiled, as if to say, "Well? Give it away."

The woman looked around the room and said, "Who here needs this camera?" A young film student looked up, and she was immediately drawn to give it to him. She did not receive another camera during the conference, but the room was electrified by seeing the principle in action. A giving frenzy ensued. People started asking each other what they needed. If they had something that met another's need, they freely gave it away.

It became clear to all of us there that often, we are to release the miracle of God's provision to one another. And when we do, God sees our joyful giving (or even our reluctant giving done in secret), and He rewards us openly, abundantly, with a good measure overflowing to us and through us.

As we stumble into our destiny, we all learn somewhere along the line that it is more blessed to give than to receive. Eventually, we also realize that we never own anything except what the Lord gives us. We can only do so much on our own to reach our destiny. The rest depends on God. Only He can make us into so much more than who we have become.

# 10

## EXPERIENCING GOD'S FINANCIAL MIRACLES

Once upon a time, we believed that we could attain the American dream if we worked hard enough. We believed our own hands and intellect created wealth. We had no need to "live by faith"—or so we thought.

The truth is, we have always lived by faith and by God's grace. And now God is calling us to upgrade our relationship with Him and to learn to trust Him for our daily bread and for strategies to create wealth supernaturally. In difficult economic times, we lose confidence in ourselves and in our own ability to provide. However, we have the potential to gain confidence in God's ability to provide. He can teach us to fly beyond our limitations and soar on the winds of faith with Him. While the earth shakes under economic duress, we Christians must come to recognize that God is the God of more than enough.

Times may come when we do not have the financial resources on hand to meet our bills or care for our children's needs or the needs of those for whom God has made us responsible. The bank account runs low. We are in a day and age when retirement accounts have shrunk due to mismanagement or outright theft. Businesses are going bankrupt. People are losing their homes. Various cities, states and even nations scramble to cover their debts and meet their payrolls. Even those with money discover that money has its limitations—there are some things money cannot buy.

In the movie *Hook*, Robin Williams plays a grown-up Peter Pan. The Peter who once could fly has now become an attorney with a family of his own. He is confident in his own ability to provide for his family, but there comes a day when he faces a spiritual battle with lives at stake and discovers that his money is worthless in that context. His archenemy—Captain Hook—has resorted to kidnapping Peter's children to lure him back to Neverland for a final battle. It is a huge wake-up call that stirs Peter toward remembering who he is and who he is destined to be.

But when Peter does wake up, he cannot remember his childhood. Nor can he cope with the fact that he must do something drastic to save his family. So in one scene, he is in the playroom pouring himself a drink and wandering around self-medicating, trying to figure out how to get his kids back. For a long moment, he stares out the window, as if his children will miraculously fly back into the room.

Suddenly, from out of the night sky, this orb of light flies at the tipsy Peter, who backs away from the window and swats at what he thinks is a giant firefly. It is Tinker Bell. Yet Peter does not remember her. She desperately tries to remind him of his adventures with pirates, sleeping in the wild, the freedom of childhood. Peter, still resisting, thinks he is having a nervous breakdown. Eventually, she manages to knock him out and whisk him away to Neverland. In a sense, she penetrates the thin place between heaven and earth, flies through the veil and takes Peter with her.

188

I have always seen Tinker Bell as a representation of the Holy Spirit in this story, so it is as if the Holy Spirit is saying, "Remember when the world was ours—we could do anything!"

I see Peter as having a visitation from heaven in this movie—a spiritual experience of sorts. Tinker Bell invites him to come with her, and he replies, "I'm seeing a white light, I must be dying." But he is starting to have an encounter that will take him into the other realm, which resembles death. He thinks he is having a mental breakdown, though. Tinker Bell pulls the rug out from underneath him and wraps him in the bedsheet, and he is so groggy that he says, "I'm seeing stars."

So Tinker Bell (think Holy Spirit in spiritual terms) flies him away to the second star on the right, which means now he is being dragged off into a visitation. Riding the glory dust, Tinker Bell flies Peter up past time, London's famous Big Ben clock, and moves outside the city gates, over the London Bridge and into a visitation that coincides with his mission—to save his children. As he enters into his destiny, other people on the bridge start to rise into the glory realm by default, just because Peter is passing through in glory.

Immediately after Tink drops Peter in Neverland, onto the dock where Captain Hook's pirate ship is moored, she says, "Get down, get low and hide." All of a sudden, Peter is in this different portal of eternity. He is actually thrown right into the enemy's camp, and he starts to see where the fight lies. Unfortunately, Peter has forgotten how to fight. He does not even understand he is in spiritual warfare, so Tinker Bell (again think Holy Spirit) disguises him to look like one of the pirates and tells him to walk out there.

When Peter observes Hook boasting of kidnapping his children to use as bait, he gets so angry that he reveals himself. Hook does not believe that Peter, whom he calls a "pasty-faced codfish," is really his former arch-nemesis, Peter Pan.

In other words, the fight is still on between Peter Pan and Captain Hook. There is no truce. The enemy is out there saying, "I'm going to kill you any way I can. If I've got to kill your children first and then kill you, I will."

Peter does what any attorney, accountant or businessman would do—he takes out his pen rather than his sword and grabs his checkbook, thinking money will win over war. However, Hook wants revenge, not cash. He is after blood, and only Peter's will do.

Money is not going to work in this battle. Hook takes out his gun and puts a bullet through the checkbook, then commands his crew to raise the net with Peter's kids trapped inside it. Raising the stakes, Hook challenges Peter to fly up to the highest yardarm of the ship to touch the hands of his children, who are suspended high above the deck. Alas, Peter has forgotten how to fly. His children are crestfallen that their father seems so powerless before the enemy. The ship's crew is aghast that Peter has forgotten his identity and the faith of his childhood that enabled him to do great exploits. To save his children, Peter must remember how to fly.

Eventually, Peter transcends his attorney mindset and enters into a new awareness of the heavenly realms accessed by childlike faith and happy thoughts. He flies beyond the realm of the material and partners with heaven's supernatural provision, so to speak. In the end, he saves himself and his children. Money has no more hold over him because he knows that wealth was of no use at all in his battle. His eyes have opened to the fact that he was fighting not against flesh and blood nor financial concerns. His enemy was of another world—as was the help Peter needed to defeat him.

Neither is our enemy flesh and blood, nor corporate takeovers nor economic recessions. We live in the middle of an ongoing spiritual battle, and our enemy does to us the same thing Captain Hook did to Peter—the enemy of our souls tends to fire a bullet right through our checkbooks when we believe we need our money the most.

Financial woes and blows are often expressions of supernatural warfare. The natural things (like the economy) speak of the invisible (like war in the heavens). In our current economic recession and in the ones to come, all of us will come to realize that we live by faith—and many will come into supernatural ideas of how to create wealth, as well as experience jaw-dropping moments of miraculous provision, both financial and material. They will discover that they have learned to fly—on the winds of the Holy Spirit.

But you have to meet some conditions if you are to experience God's miraculous provision and overcome the evil one's intent. Your arch-nemesis wants to bankrupt you and leave you so full of fear and financial insecurity that you find yourself too paralyzed to believe that you were meant to fly. To win the battle, you need to meet a couple conditions:

The first condition is to develop a friendship with God.

The second condition is to learn to give.

In the meantime, you can find God's promise to you in Paul's words, "You will be made rich in every way so that you can be generous on every occasion, and through us your generosity will result in thanksgiving to God" (2 Corinthians 9:11).

### From Ordinary to Extraordinary

God wants to move us from receiving ordinary provision to living in extraordinary prosperity. But there is one qualification for those who live by God's value system: Are you willing to sow into the Kingdom or even to give it all away? God values relationship with you first. God's prosperity positions us for a higher purpose—the purpose of being generous to others,

God's prosperity positions us for a higher purpose—the purpose of being generous to others.

191

overcoming the work of the enemy that has "Hooks" in our lives and in our communities, and working to increase the rule and reign of Jesus on earth as it is in heaven.

There are times when we move from sustaining provision into great prosperity. If we live in God's value system, we begin to learn that love has both emotional expressions and material expressions. Financial prosperity positions us to either hoard up wealth for ourselves and live comfortably in this life or release greater expressions of God's love toward others.

Jesus told one rich young man to give all his wealth away if he wanted to consider himself a follower of Jesus. But the young man chose instead to walk away from following God and retain his wealth in this lifetime—forsaking the true wealth that could have been his (see Matthew 19:16–24). He valued his money over a relationship with Jesus. Yet others who had nothing to give moved from dungeons to throne rooms. In the Old Testament, Joseph, the promised wonder boy who was supposed to be rich and famous, lingered instead in prison. While in prison, Joseph learned to live on the currency of God's love. Drawing on his faith to survive, his spirit soared into the heavens and brought back gifts to earth—gifts that became prophetic strategies that purchased favor with the earthly king who eventually released him from prison and turned the kingdom over to him.

Having learned about the currency of God's love, Joseph could then be trusted to act not just for his own sake. His actions had once been those of an impulsive, egotistical favorite son, but he had gone on to learn that godliness with contentment is a greater gain. He had learned to forgive as well and had realized that his purpose for gaining wealth was to become a wise steward of it and provide for others in their time of desperate need. His prison became the gateway to prosperity for a purpose higher than feeding his own ego or his own family. His prosperity then transformed nations— because he had learned to develop a deep relationship with God while hidden away in the prison of life, and he had also learned to love and to give generously. Joseph's prosperity also revealed God's love of nations as well as individuals. God desires to reach out to lost tribes and unbelieving nations through you and me.

For several months, I found myself working a consulting job that had me on the road for months at a time, living in hotel rooms, pouring my life out for others. During that season I saved what I could, hoping to end my days as a renter and buy my own house. Eventually, I decided to give up my rental house, put my stuff in storage and hit the road full-time for a season so that I could pay off debt and find my dream home. After a couple months of watching my bank account rise, I felt elated. My joy in coming one step closer to my dream every day dampened the distressing, horribly lonely and dietarily disastrous lifestyle of hotel living. Then one day, I received an email from a missionary couple whom I knew and liked, who worked with children in Africa. I thought nothing of sending them a nice, big donation. And that was the beginning of my realization that God was calling me not to hoard, but to give.

We are called both to create wealth and to give. The emotional battle for control over our own checkbooks is also a spiritual one. Mike Bickle, founder of the International House of Prayer ministry in Kansas City, Missouri, has much to say about this financial battle. He is a man who has learned to make wealth by listening to the strategy of the Lord, and to give quickly and easily when the Lord says give.

Mike knows that the world is shaking . . . financial institutions and world governments struggle to survive, while the rich get richer and the poor get poorer. He also knows that God's Word reveals that He can command the ravens to feed you. God will supply where there is no supply. The silver and the gold are His. The enemy may shoot your checkbook and retirement account, but God will win the war. And He promises never to leave you nor forsake you.

In a series Mike taught about finances before our most recent recession became fully acknowledged in the media,

Mike stated, "There is a great shaking coming—to the nations, economy, etc. We will see the greatest harvest worldwide in the coming decades. Haggai 2 and Hebrews 12 talk about this. God will manifest everything as unreliable except Him. In Luke, it says their hearts will fail because of fear. Fear will dominate unbelievers with the redemptive purpose resulting in them coming to Him.

"God will reveal Himself as the only reliable source that can be trusted. In the midst of the shaking, every country will be shaken economically. God's power will be supernaturally released in the area of finances."[1]

## Financial Miracles Happen

We are already hearing stories of God's ability to release finances. Sometimes He moves the heart of a person to open his or her bank account and give to meet a need. At other times, money seems to rain down supernaturally from heaven.

Larry Krieder, a leader of the house church movement in the U.S. and author of several books, told me the story of walking out his front door one morning and noticing what seemed to be pieces of paper littered all over his lawn. Investigating further, he was overjoyed to discover that his green lawn was covered by greenbacks!

"I never knew where it came from, but we didn't question it," Larry said. "We just gathered it up and thanked God for His miraculous provision. It hasn't happened since. It only happened that one time, but it sure blew in at a needed time."

Stephen DeSilva handles much of the financial work for a rather large church called Bethel Church in northern California. Like most CPAs, he feels responsible for paying the bills—all of them, on time. During one season in church life, giving was down and payday was upon them. He needed money and he needed it fast. Little did he know that God had already moved the heart of a believer to meet the need:

I was wondering what to do. The checkbook lay open on the floor before me as I walked in circles. Praying and speaking aloud, I explained to God, *"This is not a drill. I really need a miracle right now! Please provide the money!"* I didn't know how this faith-thing worked. Faced with what felt like an imminent disaster, all I could do was walk in circles and petition.

I was raising the fervent prayer of James 5:16, hoping to remind God of this obscure section of Scripture; perhaps He had forgotten and needed my gentle reminder. *I'm righteous by Your blood, and this is as fervent as I know how to get.* It was Wednesday. The coming Friday called for a $30,000 payday, and we were a mere $10,000 of the way there, just enough to cover the missionary and tithe commitments owed today.

Asking Bill, the senior pastor, what to do, he suggested that we pray. "It has come to that," he joked. I smiled unenthusiastically and tried on a meager courtesy laugh. After prayer, he directed me to pay the tithe and missionaries. "We'll pray in the rest," he said. "God may still provide somehow."

"Shouldn't I use what we have to cover some of the payroll? These people have entrusted their livelihood to us. I feel so responsible for them," I told him.

He responded that it was the same with the missionaries, and their due date was upon us. We would take care of the immediate commitments before us and seek God for the rest.

This was the backdrop of this moment of truth. Would God provide in time?

While I whined and moaned and imagined the worst, I continued to express my desperation in the form of prayers. When I was spent, I wandered back to my office, too distracted to work on anything else. As I sat down in my chair, my telephone buzzed—someone was here to see me. "Let them in," I said.

A church member stood before me, smiled and handed me a check for $35,000. He went on to tell me how he had been trying to deliver this gift for three months. "Problems kept coming up, and cash flow struggles held it back. But today, here it is. I hope you can use it. See you later." With that, he stepped out of my office and into my heart's hall of fame.

I sat and wept tears of thanks for God's deliverance. There was no possible way this person could have known the situation we faced, yet the check exactly matched the payroll, plus payroll tax deposits needed the next day. The provision had come in after our payment of the $10,000 to missionaries and tithes. My prayers had been passionate in the crisis, but God had established our deliverance three months prior, before I even knew of the need. I have never before or since seen God's hand as miraculously and hilariously demonstrated as on that day. Jesus, ever the miracle Man, continues to display His signs and wonders to those who will watch and learn.[2]

God stretched the faith of Stephen and his pastor to receive what was needed to meet their church payroll. The $30,000 they needed seems like small change now compared with how much growth the church has gone through in the ensuing decade and how large their biweekly payroll is today. But the faith-building lesson reminded Steve that he was not responsible to meet the financial burden—the burden was the Lord's.

Time after time, people speak about receiving financial miracles—both large and small—right at the needed time. Whether you need $35,000 or a windfall from heaven, God is more than able to supply what you need from sources you never dreamed of. Watch and pray. It may happen today.

### Power to Create Wealth

While God can and does move sovereignly to meet our needs, God also promises that He will give us the power to produce wealth.

## Promise

*You may say to yourself, "My power and the strength of my hands have produced this wealth for me." But remember the LORD your God, for it is he who gives you the ability to produce wealth, and so confirms his covenant, which he swore to your forefathers, as it is today.*

Deuteronomy 8:17–18

It is a promise that contains a condition. The promise is that God will give you the supernatural ability to create wealth. The condition is that you remember that your ideas are really God ideas—they originate with Him. He gives supernatural power to create wealth, relative to each one's "talent." Someone who makes $30,000 a year may create an extra $5000. A wealthy man may become a millionaire many times over. A housewife may act on a God idea and bring in an extra thousand dollars or thousands of dollars. Wealth is a relative term. An extra $100 is a fortune to a poor, penniless college student but is nothing to the CEO of a Fortune 500 company.

How do you and I get this ability to create wealth? We go to the Source. As we upgrade our relationship with Jesus, we begin hearing Him speak very personally. Sometimes, God's miraculous provision begins with a hunch. Then it is up to you and me to follow through. A hunch may lead us to take action. And at the end of the day, when the hunch pays off, we face one of two options—believing that the hunch originated with us, or trusting that the idea originated with God and we acted on it in faith.

Ray Smith is a businessman who lives in upstate Louisiana. I met him and his wife, Lynn, while on a short-term mission trip in Brazil. His nametag not only stated where he was from, but included his occupation. Ray billed himself as a "farmer" and told us that his family had a large orange grove just outside New Orleans. During that trip, we anxiously watched the images streaming across the Internet of Hurricane Katrina ravaging New Orleans and wreaking havoc along the coastline of Louisiana and Mississippi. We also listened in awe when Ray calmly announced, "I just received an email that my orange grove is totally gone."

We all felt horrible about his loss. When I turned to him to express my sympathy, his next reply made me realize why Ray was so calm. "Ahhh, Jew-yah, I'm blessed," he drawled (pronouncing *Julia* as only a Southerner can). "The orange grove will take years to come back, but mah-yah real crop is o'l and gas." His underground farm was intact.

Eventually, as I got to know Ray and Lynn, I would understand that his calm demeanor did not stem from his assurance that his oil and gas speculations would withstand disaster. His peace rose from a deeper source. He knew that he had an anointing for business, yet he was keenly aware that the senior partner was God, with His unfathomable wisdom and knowledge. So long as Ray maintained a prayerful posture and listened to God, he knew that his business would go well no matter what the economy or the weather.

Ray explained about the secrets to his successful partnership with the Lord: "I am a man of the Presence. Because of an intimate relationship with the Lord, I can hear from the Lord in ways others cannot—I just need to be obedient to follow through. I have learned that when you get into a business deal or bad times, if you begin to operate out of fear, you are operating out of the wrong spirit. When everyone was losing money in the stock market, my stock profile was doing better. Rather than selling off, I actually bought. When you are in the business world and you are connected to the Lord, you've got to operate in the Presence. You don't let a downturn bother you."

It is a partnership that has paid off through the years, as Ray has trusted the "hunches" the Lord has given him during prayer. Eventually, Ray realized that he had gained an anointing for business. God was blessing him and retraining him by teaching him biblical, relational models for success.

"What caused me to realize that you could have an anointing for business was reading Ed Silvoso's books," Ray added. "His central theme was about doing business in a whole different way. He wrote that you should approach making money not by thinking about how much you want to make, but by thinking about what you could live on reasonably well, and then why don't you just think about giving stuff away? I read that and said, *Lord, I want to go there with You.*"

Ray was so inspired that he pulled out his calculator and figured out how much they needed to live on. He took that figure to the Lord in prayer, and he heard the Lord change the plan.

"The Lord gave me a different dollar amount to live on and said, *Give Me the rest.* So I made that deal with the Lord. We call them covenants, but essentially a covenant is a deal," Ray said.

It was not long after Ray made the deal with God that God began releasing a greater sense of His presence when Ray took his business questions to Him. Ray learned to discern when God prompted him to act and when God held him back. Ray has made many successful deals since then.

"Very soon after that deal with God, I had the opportunity to buy an oil and gas mineral package. God gave me a plan of action and a percent to buy. The number he gave me was 5 percent. After we owned it about a year, several people who were in the deal with us started complaining that we were holding onto it too long. They just wanted to flip it. But I knew the Lord had a destiny for this and told them that we shouldn't sell yet. Within a few months after that, a large company offered us about three times as much as we had invested. That was not to buy it—that was just an option to lease it. We sold them an option to lease it for three times as much, and we had almost gotten our money back on that investment anyway."

Ray's deal with God is one that he is keeping. Much of the overflow from it now goes into missions.

"It is not like I'm thinking about church teachings on tithing anymore. God shows us where to give, and we have to keep our hands open. We have to be willing to listen to His leading, stop and pray and see what the Lord would have us give."

Over time, Ray's business associates have become accustomed to the possibility that they can hear from the Lord on business deals. And they, too, have been influenced to try out that spiritual promise—give and it will be given to you . . . a good measure . . . an oil gusher full . . . uncapped . . . unstoppable . . . spilling over to the nations.

## Learning to Give and Receive

After speaking in a Sunday morning service at a friend's church in Nova Scotia, Canada, I met another extraordinary businessman who is first and foremost a "man of the Presence," working with CEO Jesus for the benefit of the Kingdom worldwide. George (not his real name) is a humble, ordinary-looking man in his early sixties who lives with his wife in Nova Scotia. Early in the morning, he sits in his living room, listening to the Lord and receiving inventions and business strategies that are changing third-world nations. If I had not stopped to chat with George after the service, I never would have known what a gift he is to the world.

He told me that one of his more recent products is transforming communities in several countries. The product he developed was an advanced concrete composite that is lighter in weight than ordinary concrete and not only bulletproof, but also wind, fire, insect and mold resistant—perfect for creating prefab building panels. The panels can be shipped in bulk to any country or mixed onsite. They are used to build housing communities quickly, with the goal in mind of providing long-term, sustainable housing solutions. The motto of the company that now produces the concrete is "to put babies and families into safe and happy homes."

The early version of the product was used as a building panel system for housing and community infrastructure projects in Costa Rica, Malaysia and Venezuela. Once the communities are in place, the company tithes 10 percent of its profits back into the community to assist with building the internal resources its citizens will need. This system is so successful that the Canadian government has subcontracted for the company to build communities in other nations as well.

Housing needs remain a huge concern in many parts of the world, but developing sustainable agriculture for food and creating safe sources of drinking water will continue to play an even more vital role in the decades to come. One morning, George took the issue to the Lord during his prayer time. It was not long before he received two key ideas. Acting on both ideas, he researched the food shortage problems facing farmers in the decimated areas of the Amazon rain forest, where the slash-and-burn techniques of clearing the timber made the land unusable for farming or regrowth of trees. He soon discovered that the nutrients necessary for sustaining food growth lay not far beneath the soil's surface—yet still too deep to allow seeds to germinate or to support any significant agricultural endeavor. He took the matter to the Lord and received the idea for a nonchemical, organic process that would raise the nutrients into the topsoil. He is currently working with the Brazilian and Canadian governments to help restore the land.

In the meanwhile, George also received a download of revelation about how to desalinate large quantities of water without using nuclear energy, by using a settlement process of eliminating the sediments—a less expensive and more accessible process for many small nations.

This businessman is truly someone who has learned to give—first to the Lord, and then to others with a Kingdom mindset. Prosperity and provision have then been given to him in abundance. God found a man He could trust with riches not just for himself, but for the nations.

No matter what field they work in or what they do in life, those who give always discover that they receive even more.

## Beyond Basic Provision

George and Ray are being blessed financially as they focus first on their relationship with Jesus, partnering with Him in all they do, then on giving where God directs them to give. But what of others involved in business or ministry who do not seem to be able to create wealth? Why does it seem that they cannot move from receiving basic provision for the journey to prospering abundantly?

Mike Bickle, of the International House of Prayer, believes that one of the main reasons God does not bless people financially is because leaders have not called the Church to focus on one divine promise in particular—"Give, and it will be given to you" (Luke 6:38). Like the two businessmen I just mentioned, many people give beyond a tenth of their profits (a biblical tithe) to the work of the ministry. Some even give beyond the local church in order to impact the world. Those are the people who are blessed in their finances, but they had to start somewhere.

Mike Bickle offers us a way into receiving the promise of provision and the secret to prospering. He says, "Begin a journey of developing a history in God where He empowers you with power encounters in the realm of finances for the sake of the Kingdom. I remember times when I sowed into the Kingdom of God, and He gave a corresponding answer. He showed me that He heard my voice, saw my deeds and acted on my behalf . . . it is an amazing power encounter when that happens!"

As a young man working in youth ministry, Mike had little money of his own. He learned that as he gave $10 to someone, the Lord often gave him $20 in return. It was as if the Lord was teaching Mike how to give generously and willingly, taking no thought for himself in his willingness to obey the prompting of the Holy Spirit to give. Eventually, Mike stepped out in faith and promised to pay for several students to attend a ski retreat. Mike had no money, but he asked God to back him up and supply the funds for these students. Just as the group had packed up the bus and it was about ready to leave the church parking lot, a man walked up to Mike and handed him several $50 bills, then started to walk away. Mike was elated when he counted the money, but immediately he realized that he was still $50 short of what he needed. Suddenly the man stopped, dug into his wallet for another bill and turned back to give it to Mike. It was the final $50 that he needed.

"I've learned that there needs to be a lifestyle of giving before you give bigger. I went from giving $10 and receiving $20, to paying for college kids to go on a retreat," Mike explained. But the lesson on giving did not end with that realization. Giving released something more in Mike—a greater depth of relationship built on trust.

"When the invisible God shows that He is listening to you, caring about you, considering your actions and acting according to your actions, you begin to look up, and you don't feel alone anymore. When the concept hit me that God did something because I asked Him to, it was amazing," Mike concluded.[3]

Giving enables you to know God as your Source, the One who provides more than enough for you so that you may have more than enough to give to others.

## Receiving God's Miraculous Provision

So many people have no history of watching God release finances or provision for them, so they grow faint with fear when economic woes come. They do not know God as their source. They have only relied on themselves or social services and government programs to assist them. And when all of that fails, the only place they can look is up.

He wants all of us to experience encounters with Him that elevate our faith and trust. When the going gets really tough in North America, it may be that no one prospers and food resources become ravaged by climate change. It may be that our economy plummets into a second Great Depression, and it may be that third-world church leaders will end up showing us the way to access the very miracles they have received over the years. Third-world church leaders have learned that true prosperity is not financial—it is spiritual, found in the wealth of our relationship with Jesus Christ and deepened through love.

Missionaries and aid agencies fly tons of food every week into remote areas in third-world countries to feed victims of famine caused by droughts, poor agricultural practices and flooding. Sometimes, the food does not make it to its destination or gets rerouted to another location. Some days, missionaries stand and cry tears of despair as they face the masses of starving children, knowing that they have nothing—not even a loaf of bread for their own children to eat. And they look to Jesus and say, "Where will we get enough bread to feed such a crowd?"

Heidi Baker, a missionary in Mozambique, knows the answer to that question. She has been there, and through the years she has learned not to weep in despair, but to rejoice, knowing that her Father always provides. When the sights and sounds, the tears of the masses overwhelm her; when thousands stand in front of her seeking food; when the overwhelming sickness, open sores and smells of death assault her, she redirects her attention onto the face of Jesus.

"Just focus on His face," she says. "You will only make it to the end if you can focus on His face. Focus on His beautiful face. You can't feed the poor, you can't go to the street, you can't see anything happen unless you see His face. One glance of His eyes, and we have all it takes."[4]

Once, when her Chihango Children's Ministry in Maputo faced severe persecution, the entire staff was given 48 hours to vacate their buildings and move out of town. And so they worked nonstop for 48 hours to clear out everything they could, lest it be confiscated or stolen when they left. They had no idea what to do with the children who came to their center. The children had no idea what to do, either. And so more than one hundred children followed Heidi and Rolland Baker to the gate of their small apartment; some flooded into the house, while others, with their faces pressed against the gate, just stood there. In fact, the Bakers' own two children stood amidst the chaos and exhaustion, as overwhelmed as their parents.

Heidi looked over the crowd of children inside her house and those spilling onto the street and thought she was going to snap. She had neither the food nor the pots to cook the quantities of food that these children would require. Just then, a woman from the U.S. Embassy across the street knocked on her door. She thought she would just stop in with a little dinner for the Bakers—give them some chili and rice—just enough for the four of them. Heidi relates what happened:

> We hadn't eaten in days. I opened a door and showed her all our children. "I have a big family!" I pointed out tiredly but in complete and desperate earnest. My friend got serious. "There isn't enough. I must go home and cook some more!" But I just asked her to pray over the food. . . . We began serving and right from the start I gave everyone a full bowl. I was dazed and overwhelmed. I barely understood at the time what a wonderful thing was happening. But all our children ate, the staff ate, my friend ate and even our family of four ate. . . . Because He died, there is always enough.[5]

According to additional reports given by staff and volunteers who have worked with the Bakers' ministry, the multiplication

205

of food has occurred more than once. Many people have personally witnessed these miracles.[6]

Learn to snuggle in and listen to the words the Holy Spirit whispers in your ear during your quiet time of developing your relationship with God. Begin to note the times when He met you financially or personally in some way or another. Keep your history with God close at hand. When times get tough, you can turn to the pages and say, "I remember when God met me here and supernaturally provided. Surely He will come through again!"

Your faith, developed in the hard times, will blossom in the days to come. Rather than trying to receive something more from God, you may soon discover that you have more than enough to give to others. And who knows, even if you find yourself penniless, you may be called upon to multiply food for the masses one day. His promise of provision for others may be *you*!

# Afterword

## *The Secret to Sustaining Faith*

As you wait for the *Yes* of God to intervene in your life and shift you from hearing His promise to receiving His provision, I am going to tell you the secret to sustaining faith. The secret is this—*worship*.

Worship moves you into a place of peace where you can receive His love. No matter what is going on in your life, entering into the presence of God through worship will enable you to drop the shield of anxiety, release your pent-up emotions, calm your heart and receive a peace that passes all understanding. Once that peace settles in, God's loving presence floods in. It shields you from fear of the future and enables you to enjoy His presence in the now. Focus on the face of Jesus—no matter what storm rages around you—and though the storm rages, you will no longer notice because you are captivated by Him.

Worship! David worshiped the Lord. At times, he ranted and whined in his psalms, but he always pulled up—shifting his focus from domestic problems and leadership wocs to heaven. He ended his psalms in worship, strengthening himself in the knowledge that God was with him.

Worship! Time after time, Daniel worshiped the Lord while his enemies set him up to be destroyed. And he was heard in the throne room of heaven and blessed with tremendous favor.

Worship! The apostles worshiped the Lord through the hard times and through the good times, and God heard their prayers. Before they saw the answer to their prayers, they entered into His presence, and His presence was enough for them to let go of fear and trust in His promise of provision. Their worship enabled prison doors to swing open and angels to come to their rescue. No matter how they felt physically or emotionally, they worshiped.

Worship releases an atmosphere of faith that fills our natural surroundings and circumstances. We sense that we are not alone as we feel God say to us, "Do not be afraid, for I am with you" (Isaiah 43:5).

Worship enables us to love God and begin to see the salvation of God. Worship reminds us that God is the Savior of the world—we are not. We cannot even save ourselves. We need a loving God who reminds us of who He is and gives us words, from His Word, to pray back to Him, to enable us to stir up our faith in His faithfulness. Remember what the Lord has done in your life and thank Him for that. Recall His words and remind Him of His promises. Declare that they will come to pass. And listen for His response. He will let you know that He sees your troubles, and He will strengthen you as you spend time with Him, waiting with Him in the place of worship:

> O Jacob, O Israel, how can you say that the Lord doesn't see your troubles and isn't being fair? Don't you yet understand? Don't you know by now that the everlasting God, the Creator of the farthest parts of the earth, never grows faint or weary? No one can fathom the depths of his understanding. He gives power to the tired and worn out, and strength to the weak.

Even the youths shall be exhausted, and the young men will all give up. But they that wait upon the Lord shall renew their strength. They shall mount up with wings like eagles; they shall run and not be weary; they shall walk and not faint.

Isaiah 40:27–31, TLB

There are days when God is so present to me at home that I am overcome with His love. And there have been dark hours when He seemed to have faded into the distance right when I needed Him most and when the spirit of despair settled on my shoulders like a heavy winter coat. Those dark hours tend to cause you and me to isolate ourselves rather than running to God and seeking to draw nearer to Him. It is during those dark hours that we need to seek out the places that are ablaze with His light and infused with His presence. Once there, we need to open our hearts to receive His healing.

During worship in a service or gathering and afterward, ask those in the meeting to pray for you. How badly do you want to be released from the spirit of despair and enter into the unbearable lightness of love and glory? Ask God to lead you to where His power resides and His presence draws a crowd. He will meet you there. Wait in the community of other believers, whose praise and worship can sink into your soul when you do not have the strength to sing or pray yourself. Wait, and He will come with healing and restoration.

Now that you have read the stories in this book, you can see another theme emerging: Love reveals itself more clearly in relationships and in the community of "the saints." We need each other. God often releases His miraculous provision through another person or within the atmosphere of corporate worship. And some days, you may be the one who releases God's miraculous provision to another person or even to a nation.

Worship draws us together into a community of believers and reduces us to utter dependency on His presence to sustain us, provide for us and prosper us so that we have more than enough to give to others . . . even though the bank account runs low. As we worship, our hearts align with His heart, and we become less focused on our immediate needs and move into His presence, allowing Him to be God.

In community, people begin to open up to the presence of God, and then they begin to give sacrificially as the Spirit of the Lord moves them. It happened in the book of Acts, where the believers shared all their possessions with one another and took care of those in need (see Acts 2:44–46; 4:32–35). And it happened in the Patricia King meeting that I described in chapter 9. God is able to supply whatever we need for today and for tomorrow. When we offer a sacrifice of praise when we feel like crying, our hearts begin to transcend the pain. We offer a sacrifice of giving to another, and we feel His pleasure at our gift given in secret. And He gives us more. Give, and it shall be given to you . . . a good measure, pressed down . . . running over. . . . In the words of the late John Wimber, "We give to get; and get to give."

## A Glimpse of Jesus

You can also find another common theme emerging from the stories in this book: Life is hard at times, and we all grow weary, but God is always good and always provides. He provides beyond wealth, and He invites you to come closer still into an encounter with Him that will steady your faith and revive your love:

> Come to me, all you who are weary and burdened, and I will give you rest. Take my yoke upon you and learn from me, for I am gentle and humble in heart, and you will find rest for your souls. For my yoke is easy and my burden is light.
>
> Matthew 11:28–30

When Jesus said this, He had just finished talking about three cities He had visited. In Korazin, Bethsaida and Capernaum, He went about healing the sick, raising the dead, casting out demons and setting the people free from their burdens. The residents in those places romped in the light of His presence and received His gifts, then turned and walked back into their old routines, their old thoughts and behaviors—back into their bondage. They failed to follow Him. But once again, Jesus offered them more of Himself and cried out, "Come to me . . . and I will give you rest." We who are still on this side of eternity are sometimes no different than they were, and yet He keeps calling us, too.

He is gentle and humble of heart. His desire is for you to enter into rest, peace and joy. His desire is for you to lay down your burden and become connected to Him (yoked together) until you are walking in step with Him, joined at the hip, so to speak.

Jesus offers a choice—you can come under the yoke of slavery, where you are oppressed by the enemy's tormenting thoughts and religious demands, or by the fears and despair that settle in during personal and economic troubles—or you can come and be God's beloved son or daughter, released to live within the presence of His love.

His longing is for you to lay down your burden, the faults that your conscience uses to oppress your soul or the circumstances of life in a fallen world that oppress you, and come under His burden, His authority, a light place to be. He does not call you to walk alone under a heavy weight of depression or crushing anxiety, under the oppression of the enemy. The burden Jesus offers is one of coming under the authority of His gentle love.

Who is this Jesus?

- He is "gentle and humble" (Matthew 11:29).
- "He does not treat us as our sins deserve" (Psalm 103:10).
- He "is not a man, that he should lie, nor a son of man, that he should change his mind. Does he speak

and then not act? Does he promise and not fulfill?" (Numbers 23:19).

Your Savior is crying out to you, "Come, My beloved! And I will give you rest!" Take time to meet with Him here and now, and whisper this prayer out loud:

Jesus, my gentle and humble friend, I hear You calling my name.
So I come to You now, lay down my burden, drop it at Your feet and say,
Here I am. Come be with me.
Come, fill me with an awareness of how very near You are to me.
Come into my life and give me a glimpse of You. Reveal Yourself to me.
Forgive all my sins and heal all my diseased thoughts and behaviors.
Heal my heart, mind, body and soul.
I surrender to You—God of love who never lies.
I trust You—God who fulfills promises.
I worship You, my Savior and my friend.
I receive Your peace and rest.

And now, listen. For this is His response, whispered to me for you:

### A Love Note from Papa

My dear one,
Nothing can separate you from My love.
Nothing can separate you from My healing, from My provision, from My presence, from My glory.
I am not a god in heaven who waits for sacrifice and withholds blessing until I am satisfied. I do not withhold Myself from you or anyone else. I am the Now, the Yes and Amen.
I run in response to faith. I respond every time you turn your eyes to Me. I speak every time you sit and listen. I am here.

212

I Am!

Desperate people lay hold of the hem of My garment and find healing. Lovers sit with Me and linger long in My presence. Paupers receive the wisdom to become kings when they seek Me and hear and act. Those who gather together in unity experience My presence even more expansively, for I am there in their midst. Even those who come alone will experience My provision and presence beyond measure. I am here.

I am Jehovah Rapha, your healer.

I am Jehovah Shalom, your peace.

I am Jehovah Shamah, the one who is there and hears your whispered prayer.

I am Jehovah Jirah, your provider.

Come . . . and be with Me.

Enter into My grace for the journey.

Love,

Abba

# NOTES

## Chapter 1: He Hears Your Whispered Prayers

1. For more about Taylor and David Causer, visit www.miraculouslove.com.

## Chapter 3: Angels Watching over You

1. For more about Shawn Bolz, visit www.expression58.org.
2. For more about the late Jill Austin, visit www.masterpotter.com.

## Chapter 4: Hope beyond Reason for Healing

1. Dave Hess, *Hope Beyond Reason: Embraced by God's Presence in the Toughest of Times* (Shippensburg, Penn.: Destiny Image, 2008), 44–46.
2. Ibid., 72–73.
3. Ibid., 74–76.
4. Ibid., 147–49.
5. For more about Dave and Sheri Hess, visit www.christcc.org.
6. Ibid., 159–60.

## Chapter 6: He Crowns Your Family with Salvation

1. For more about Allison Moseley, visit www.rootedandgrounded.com.
2. For more about Barbara Yoder, visit www.shekinahchurch.org.
3. For more about Paul Keith Davis, visit www.whitedoveministries.org.

## Chapter 7: The Blessing of Childlike Faith

1. Jennifer Toledo, as quoted at www.globalchildrensmovement.org, where you can find out more about Jennifer and the ministry she directs.
2. For more about Judy Franklin, visit www.ibethel.org.

## Chapter 8: Recovering Commitments to Marriage and Ministry

1. For more about Kim and Mary Andersson, visit www.christ-the-rock.org.

2. Excerpted in part from Michal Ann's chapter "Visitation Encounters" in James Goll and Michal Ann Goll, *God Encounters: The Prophetic Power of the Supernatural to Change Your Life* (Shippensburg, Penn.: Destiny Image, 2005), 77–89.

3. For more about Michal Ann and James Goll, visit www.encountersnetwork. com.

## Chapter 9: Stumbling into Destiny

1. Bill Johnson, *When Heaven Invades Earth* (Shippensburg, Penn.: Destiny Image, 2005), 113.

2. Ibid., 114.

3. For more about Bill Johnson, visit www.ibethel.org.

4. For more about Patricia King, visit www.extremeprophetic.com.

## Chapter 10: Experiencing God's Financial Miracles

1. Mike Bickle's complete teaching "Experiencing Power Encounters in Finances" is available in MP3 format at www.ihopmp3store.com/Store/Products/1000002405/ All_MP3s/Teaching_Series/Speaker/Mike_Bickle/Experiencing_Power_Encounters. aspx. For more about Mike Bickle, visit www.ihop.org.

2. For more about Stephen DeSilva, visit www.prosproussoul.org.

3. Bickle, "Experiencing Power Encounters in Finances." MP3. For more about Mike Bickle, visit www.ihop.org.

4. Rolland Baker and Heidi Baker, *There Is Always Enough: The Miraculous Move of God in Mozambique* (Lancaster, UK: Sovereign World, 2003), 176–77.

5. Ibid., 5.

6. For more about Heidi and Rolland Baker, visit www.irismin.org.

Julia C. Loren is a former journalist with a B.A. from the University of Washington, a counselor with an M.S. from Seattle Pacific University and the author of several books. A native of California, she met the Lord while studying Hebrew on a very Zionist kibbutz in Israel and has the unusual testimony of being led to Jesus through the efforts of non-Messianic Jews. She has also spent many years living in the Pacific Northwest. Julia is a powerful and anointed speaker who ministers in churches and at retreats around the world. She is also a "backdoor prophet" whose behind-the-scenes ministry has blessed hundreds of leaders from all walks of life.

Julia's books include:

- *Shifting Shadows of Supernatural Power*, with contributing authors Bill Johnson, Mahesh Chavda and Graham Cooke (Destiny Image, 2006).
- *Shifting Shadows of Spiritual Experiences*, with coauthor James Goll (Destiny Image, 2007).
- *Breaking the Spirit of Despair* and *Dancing in the Fullness of Joy*, both part of the Glimpses of Jesus series—interactive journals based on glimpses of Jesus that heal and restore (Tharseo Publishing, 2006).
- *Divine Intervention: True Stories of Heaven Invading Earth* (Tharseo Publishing, 2008).
- *The Note on the Mirror: Pregnant Teenagers Tell Their Stories* (Zondervan, 1990).

- *Engel v. Vitale: Prayer in the Public Schools* (Lucent Books, 2000).

You can learn more about Julia and her books by visiting her websites at www.julialoren.net or www.divineinterventionbooks.com. You can also contact Julia by email at juliascribes@yahoo.com.